Best Story Wins

Also in the Economist Edge series

Branding That Means Business
by Matt Johnson and Tessa Misiaszek

Innovating with Impact
by Ted Ladd and Alessandro Lanteri

Giving Good Feedback
by Margaret Cheng

Best Story Wins

Storytelling for business success

Mark Edwards

BEST STORY WINS

Published with permission from *The Economist* by Pegasus Books.

The Economist is an imprint of
Pegasus Books, Ltd.
148 West 37th Street, 13th Floor
New York, NY 10018

ISBN: 978-1-63936-644-6

10 9 8 7 6 5 4 3 2 1

Printed in the United States of America
Distributed by Simon & Schuster
www.pegasusbooks.com

PEGASUS BOOKS
NEW YORK LONDON

To Sue, Sylvia and Georgia

About the author

Mark Edwards is a corporate coach who has helped his clients win over $10 billion worth of new business pitches as a pitch doctor in the media, marketing and advertising industries.

He began his career as a business journalist and for 25 years his writing appeared on a weekly basis in the *Sunday Times*. He is the co-author of *Belonging: The Key to Transforming and Maintaining Diversity, Inclusion and Equality at Work* and the author of *The Tao of Bowie: 10 Lessons from David Bowie's Life to Help You Live Yours*.

Praise for Mark Edwards's previous books:

Belonging: The Key to Transforming and Maintaining Diversity, Inclusion and Equality at Work

"The most important business book of the year" – *Esquire*

"Takes a complex and often uncomfortable subject and makes it truly accessible and absolutely achievable" – Sarah Jenkins, managing director, Saatchi & Saatchi

"Essential reading" – Mark Thompson, former president and CEO, *The New York Times*

The Tao of Bowie: 10 Lessons from David Bowie's Life to Help You Live Yours

"Quirky wisdom" – *Independent*

"A swirling, entertaining path of self-discovery" – *Publishers Weekly*

"A wise little book which will help you find clarity and creativity" – *Stylist*

Contents

Introduction:
The power of storytelling

Understanding how important storytelling is in the modern world of work; how storytelling adds value to businesses and benefits individuals; how anyone can be a storyteller; and how you can tell one of the world's most important stories in just two words

"Who is the most powerful person in the world?"

It's a summer's day in 1994, and Steve Jobs needs a snack. He walks into the breakroom at the Redwood, California headquarters of NeXT, the company he founded after being forced out of Apple. He grabs a bagel, turns to the others in the room, and asks them to name the most powerful person in the world. It's not standard breakroom banter, but this is the boss talking, so a few answers are offered, including major politicians of the day. "No," Jobs replies – confident in his opinions as ever. "You're all wrong! The most powerful person in the world is the storyteller."

It's arguably not the most obvious answer, so how had Jobs come to form this opinion? At the time of this exchange, Jobs was heavily invested in storytelling, both financially and personally. Having left Apple in 1985, following boardroom infighting, he had set up NeXT, but he had also funded the creation of Lucasfilm's graphics division as a standalone company and was its major shareholder. By 1994, it had been renamed Pixar and was only a year away from unveiling *Toy Story*, the first ever entirely computer-animated feature film, with Jobs credited as executive producer.

As well as investing financially in a company that would become one of the great popular storytellers of the age, Jobs was transforming himself from a man whose signature communications style had tended to be relentless logical argument into someone who had an entirely different way of communicating with the world.

According to Pixar co-founder Ed Catmull, Jobs referred to his original tactic as "just explain it to them until they understand"; and Catmull noted that "until they understand" was a time period that would sometimes stretch over several months. But Jobs was starting to see the limitations of this approach based on logical argument, and was gradually evolving a new storytelling style that, following his return to Apple in 1997, would see his keynote speeches at product launches hailed as masterclasses in communication.

In 2002, for example, when software developers wanted to continue to work with Mac OS 9 but Jobs wanted them to move onto OS 10, he didn't just explain it to them until they understood. He eschewed logical arguments and instead staged a mock funeral for the old operating system.

At the annual developer's conference in the San Jose Convention Center, dry ice filled the stage, stained glass imagery went up on the slides, Bach's Toccata and Fugue in D Minor played, and a coffin appeared. Jobs emerged with a box ostensibly containing Mac OS 9, walked solemnly over to the coffin and placed it inside. Slowly and deliberately, he closed the lid, placed a rose on top and gave a eulogy for the old system.

His speech was perfectly balanced between dignified

respect and gentle humour, exemplifying exactly the note you want the words at a funeral to hit: the deceased was wonderful, of course, but they had their little quirks, didn't they?

> Mac OS 9 was a friend to us all. He worked tirelessly on our behalf, always hosting our applications, never refusing a command, always at our beck and call, except occasionally when he forgot who he was and needed to be restarted.

Jobs's speech drove home the key point he wanted to make:

> We are here today to mourn the passing of Mac OS 9.
> Please join me in a moment of silence as we remember our old friend, Mac OS 9.

And crucially, Jobs never broke character. The audience laughed, but Jobs didn't crack a smile. This wasn't a logical argument as to why developers should support the new system. It was a new version of an age-old tale: the old system is dead; long live the new system.

Storytelling was integral to Apple's rise to become the most valuable brand in the world. The "Think different" campaign that quickly followed Jobs's return to the company derived from his belief that one of the key events in anyone's life is the moment when you realise that the world isn't fixed and that *you* can change it. This moment of awakening is at the heart of the classical storytelling form, the hero's journey, which can be found in cultures around the world. It's the moment when the hero accepts the "call to action" that sets the story in motion; the moment when the hero – who, until that point in the story, has no idea that this is in fact their destiny – actually *becomes* the hero.

As a metaphor it speaks powerfully to the transitional moments in our lives when we realise our agency, when we "grow up" and assume new responsibilities, when we define ourselves as individuals. Job's understanding of this elemental power of storytelling allowed him to harness its strength in just those two words.

Stories sell

We're not all going to change the world in the ways that Jobs and Apple did; we're not all going to build the most valuable brand in the world or revolutionise whole industries. But we *can* all reap the benefits of storytelling.

Storytelling allows you to communicate more powerfully in pretty much every work setting. It's the most effective way to get your point across whether you're standing up in front of a crowd at a conference or firing off a quick email to get a stakeholder's support for a project; whether you're constructing a PowerPoint presentation or chatting with a colleague in a lift.

It works for leaders running major corporations through transitional periods, and it works for someone trying to get their first ever job.

It works in 90-second Super Bowl TV spots, and it works in 10-second social media formats.

In 2014, readers of the *Journal of Marketing Theory and Practice* encountered the headline "What makes a Super Bowl ad super?"[1] The article was based on an analysis of 108 Super Bowl commercials, analysing exactly what kind of ads consumers liked most.

The Super Bowl ad break is one of the high points of the US advertising and marketing year; not only are the ads seen by more than 100 million people live, but they are also the subject of much social media and word of mouth discussion afterwards. So, which ads did people like the most and which were the ads that got the additional attention, views, likes, clicks and social buzz?

The secret sauce of a Super Bowl commercial, it turns out, is not sex appeal, humour, catchphrases or adorable animals. What people like and want to talk about is story. The ads that followed traditional narrative form were the most liked, and the more complete the story (the more closely they followed the conventional dramatic form that the authors of the article used as their model, and which we will encounter in Chapter 2), the more liked they were and the more talked about they were.

"Does story and likeability sell? Likeable ads are more likely to be viewed and shared multiple times, increasing viral buzz and generating greater awareness," according to the article. "Advertisers can buy consumer attention for those 30 seconds during the game. But when advertising hits social media, it is all about likability. People are drawn to and give their attention to story."

But surely – you may well be thinking – people don't have time for stories these days. After all, according to the media, we're supposed to be suffering from ever-shortening attention spans.

This is a well-worn theory, but is it true? Perhaps you've noticed that the same people who are accused of having tiny attention spans are easily able to binge-watch a whole series of a dozen 60-minute episodes of a TV drama – *if the story grips them*.

The truth is, of course, that we 21st-century human beings are perfectly able to focus our attention on one thing for a length of time if it interests us. And story is what interests us.

Eight years after their original research, the same authors conducted similar research into viral ad videos online.[2]

Their analysis of 155 online ads found that average shares and views were higher for videos that featured full story development than for videos that didn't. Even in the world of clickbait, people still like a good story.

Stories add value

Storytelling doesn't just get you shares and likes. It translates into hard cash.

Dollar Shave Club proved to be an extraordinarily successful start-up when it was bought by Unilever in 2016 for a reported $1bn. Did the deal make financial sense for Unilever? Increasingly, commentators are suggesting that it didn't. But it certainly made sense for Dollar Shave Club's founder Michael Dubin, who personally received $90m.

What was behind the exceptional price that Unilever paid?

Story.

The unconventional brand told its unconventional story with unconventional videos. One of them famously headlined "Our blades are f***ing great" featured Dubin's humorous delivery as he toured the warehouse. It made an immediate emotional connection with the audience: they were wasting money on overpriced razors and Dollar Shave Club was the answer.

The video was shot for $4,500. To give some idea of how cheap that is in the world of advertising, Gillette's annual marketing budget was recently reported in trade magazine *Marketing Week* at $600m.

At the time of the billion-dollar acquisition, Ryan Darnell, a principal at Basset Investment Group, a venture capital firm specialising in early-stage investments, explained the rationale for the high purchase price very clearly. "There are two things that drive multiples: the financial metrics and the story," he said.

It's hardly surprising, then, that so many business leaders

cite storytelling as a vital skill. "Entrepreneurs who make a difference are, in effect, professional storytellers," is Richard Branson's verdict; and, speaking of the Virgin group of companies, he noted: "We would be nothing without our story." Stewart Butterfield, co-founder of photo-sharing website Flickr and founder of team-messaging application Slack, said that:

> If there's one piece of advice I could go back to give myself, it is to concentrate on the storytelling part, on the convincing people. If you can't do that, it doesn't matter how good the product is, it doesn't matter how good the idea was for the market, or what happens in the external factors, you don't have the people believing.

Storytelling, it seems, is vital to success in business. Storytelling is also, fortunately, easier than it sounds.

Anyone can be a storyteller

You may feel that some people are just born storytellers – that it's a gift, and perhaps that it's one that you don't possess. But *anyone* can be a storyteller. Indeed, we all are storytellers in our daily lives; and we can bring those skills to the workplace.

I would even argue that, although we often encounter storytelling in the world of the Arts, storytelling itself is not an art. It's a science. Or, at least, it can be approached as one. There is a clear, proven way to create stories. There are simple rules or guidelines that anyone can follow. There is, if you like, a "best practice" for making a story.

There are books that have defined this best practice for those who want to write novels or films. The book you're holding now redefines that same best practice for those whose focus is on storytelling in the workplace.

As you read on, you will be reassured that storytelling is a

7

skill that is available to anyone. You don't have to be a natural storyteller, great writer or charismatic presenter.

The power of storytelling can be harnessed by following a simple, actionable six-step process. You can use this process (it's called SUPERB) to create stories; but you can also use the process (or elements of it) to improve the power of business communication in *any* medium – from emails to speeches, WhatsApps to one-on-ones, texts to town halls.

The SUPERB process will improve all your business communications, making you better able to influence, impact, persuade, sell, manage and lead.

How to read this book

You'll get the most out of *Best Story Wins* if you work through it in order, as each chapter builds on the knowledge learned in the previous one.

However, if you want to get straight to the SUPERB process to start building your own stories, then you can jump directly to Chapter 5. If you choose to do this, however, I urge you to look back over chapters 1, 2, 3 and 4 at a later date, as the context they bring will enhance your use of the process.

Here's how the book is structured.

Chapter 1 explains why storytelling is so extraordinarily powerful. It compares and contrasts building a logical argument – the most common way in which people try to influence others at work – with storytelling, to explain exactly why storytelling is significantly more effective. You'll see how storytelling aligns closely with the decision-making process of your audiences. And you'll examine the neuroscientific and psychological evidence that demonstrates why people who may resist your logical arguments and other forms of communication will be more open, and react more positively, to storytelling.

Before you can gain the benefits of storytelling you have to understand what a story is, and how it works. **Chapter 2 analyses the key theories and definitions of story from Aristotle to the present day**, taking in both the perennial truths of narrative form that have stood the test of time, and the new developments that have shaped our modern idea of story in the multi-media, multi-platform, utterly-spoilt-for-choice 21st century. This chapter will help you build up a comprehensive picture of what makes a story – and, importantly, what makes a *good* story.

Chapter 3 identifies the storytelling techniques that work best in a business setting. It also indicates the few aspects of storytelling that won't translate into your business communications and are best avoided. In this chapter you will learn who should be the hero of your story (spoiler alert: it isn't you), and we will explain why the writing style that gets great marks at school and college is completely inappropriate in the office.

Chapter 4 looks at the obstacles that can prevent us from telling powerful stories in a business setting, including PowerPoint, examining exactly how a piece of software has reduced so much of business communication to a boring sludge that is neither memorable nor persuasive. When you truly understand the pitfalls of PowerPoint you can avoid them, by using techniques like storytelling headlines, which will be a valuable tool in creating a sense of story throughout your communications.

Chapter 5 takes you through the six-step SUPERB storytelling model, explaining the role of each of the six steps and how they build to create effective communications that align with and engage your audiences.

The arrival of Big Data has revolutionised many businesses, but it has also led to countless horrendous communications. It's likely that some of the worst presentations and documents that you have encountered have been those heavy with data. The irony is that data can tell very powerful stories, if you let it. **Chapter 6 shows how the SUPERB model works as a tool to identify the story hidden in data.** This chapter also introduces a simple but powerful tool (*This is the slide/ paragraph where they* ...), which helps data-literate authors and presenters communicate more clearly with less data-literate audiences by seeing the material from the latter's perspective, naturally drawing the true importance of the data into language that everyone can understand.

The power of storytelling lies in its emotional connection and, having outlined technique and structure, I return to look more deeply at how the storytelling process meets an audience's emotional needs. **Chapter 7 moves your storytelling on to the next level by revealing the eight key emotional triggers that lie behind the SUPERB model.** They represent the emotional needs that most commonly have to be met for an audience to conclude that the meeting has gone well, that they want to work with a presenter, or that they have encountered an idea worth pursuing. Looked at the other way, they are the eight emotional needs which, if they are *not* met, will cause a meeting to end badly, a presentation to be stopped halfway through, a document to be consigned to the physical or virtual trashcan, or a business relationship to be terminated. This knowledge will allow you to improvise around the basic storytelling structure while still maintaining the desired emotional effect.

Chapter 8 takes the SUPERB storytelling model and shows exactly how to apply it to different business uses, including speeches, presentations, emails and documents, as well as employing it as a structure for meetings.

So, now you know a lot about storytelling, but how do you confront the blank sheet of paper or the blank screen? **Chapter 9 outlines a simple writing process for those who may not consider themselves natural writers**. Many people for whom writing is not their primary skill create problems for themselves by fundamentally misunderstanding what the writing process is. This chapter will help you to achieve clarity and effectiveness in your writing while helping you avoid the most common writing mistakes.

As well as having to write your own documents and presentations, as you move up the corporate ladder you'll increasingly find yourself having to edit the work of others. Faced with an impenetrable first draft and an author who thinks the work is a masterpiece, you have the tricky task of improving the work without destroying the confidence of its creator (especially important when its creator will shortly have to stand up in front of a large audience and present it). Chapter 9 also shows you how to edit other people's stories. It advocates the use of editing models, which allow the author and editor to compare a piece of work against a set of clear objectives, rather than get into a subjective and potentially confrontational conversation.

Chapter 10 contains the stories you need to know, because you might be asked to tell them and because understanding these stories will give you valuable self-awareness and help you in strategic decisions. This chapter shows how the SUPERB process can bring these stories to life, including your personal origin story, your company's foundation story, and stories about navigating change and overcoming challenges.

How *Best Story Wins* can help you

The SUPERB storytelling model, which lies at the heart of this book, is based on a deep dive into the principles of storytelling that reveals exactly why stories are such a powerful form of communication and gives you the tools you need to tell great stories.

But crucially, as well as helping you become better at telling stories, *Best Story Wins* shows exactly how the techniques that give stories their power can be applied to *all* forms of workplace communication. Remember: with "Think different", Apple was able to harness the archetypal power of storytelling in just two words.

On a theoretical level, this book will leave you with a clear understanding of why so much business communication fails, of how people make decisions and why storytelling is the most powerful way to influence that decision-making.

On a practical level, the storytelling skills and six-step process explained in the book can help anyone communicate more effectively in almost any work setting, from commanding the room when giving a speech or creating better presentations and pitches through to writing clearer emails and getting your point across in a casual conversation.

In other words, these are skills that most people could usefully employ pretty much every day.

On a company level, the ideas in this book can be used to help any organisation pitch for additional funding, connect with customers and prospects to drive brand awareness or market share, or communicate a mission or purpose to their stakeholders.

Because of its power to persuade and influence, the ability to tell stories adds value to individuals and organisations. Anyone can learn to become a better storyteller and storytelling also comes with a lifetime guarantee. Although the pace of change in today's workplace means that many of the skills we learn quickly become redundant, human nature doesn't change. The power of storytelling lies in its ability to make a human connection. It has successfully brought people together for thousands of years and will continue to do so.

1

Why storytelling works

Understanding how people make decisions; why storytelling is the best way to persuade them to make the decisions that *you* want them to make; and why sometimes people just won't listen to your beautifully crafted logical arguments

Our brain doesn't instinctively like facts and figures. Of course, it can do logical reasoning; it's very good at it. But it has to *work* at it. So many of us prefer not to engage in it too much without a lot of motivation (for example, the need to earn money to pay the bills).

Stories, however, come easily. They just slip in. We get them. They're not hard work at all.

When someone sends you a document or a slide deck at work you tend to hope that it's short – that they get to the point quickly. But fans of Lee Child or Agatha Christie don't complain about how many books they wrote and the onerous task of wading through them all. They lap them up and wish they'd written more.

Hang on, you might be thinking, this isn't a fair comparison. Those stories are *entertainment*. Exactly. Stories are, by design, entertaining. Over the millennia the story form has evolved to give our brain something it likes – and therefore stories interest and entertain us.

This doesn't mean that to be successful at work you have to tell stories all day long. But it does mean that if you can understand why stories work, why our brains like them so much, and then harness the elements of storytelling that are so powerful and apply them to your work, your business communications will become better.

Crucially, they will not only become more entertaining (they will, but that's not our primary objective); they will also become more persuasive.

Persuasion is at the heart of business success

Persuasion is one of the core skills that virtually everyone needs in business. A young person trying to find their first job has to persuade an interviewer or a panel to choose them over maybe hundreds of other applicants. At the other end of the career ladder, the CEO of a global organisation has to persuade thousands of people to fundamentally change the way they behave at work – whether that be adopting more inclusive practices or agreeing on a hybrid working solution that meets the needs of the business and all its people.

In between those two extremes almost everybody's day will include moments when persuasion is vital – whether it's getting agreement on a decision, persuading a client to pay on time in order to maintain vital cash flow, or simply persuading a colleague that the request in your email deserves their attention before the dozens of other requests they could choose to respond to first.

The better we are at persuasion, the smoother our day will go.

In a 1995 article economists Deirdre McCloskey and Arjo

Klamer suggested that the persuasion content of all United States economic activity could be as high as 25%.[1]

Having quoted Adam Smith ("everyone is practicing oratory on others through the whole of his life"), the authors then set about calculating exactly how much of each person's life is dedicated to the task (or at least how much of each industry's output). Would it be right to refer to their endeavour as an analysis, or is it more of a guesstimate? Certainly they deal in round figures. Public relations specialists, they decide, are 100% about persuasion, which seems unarguable; editors they rate at 75%, which seems reasonable.

Their verdict on the stock market is that it's pretty much *all* persuasion:

> The chatter in the stock market (that ideal of a marketplace) is another example of persuasion in the economy. Portfolio managers talk full-time to decide on buying or selling. Stockbrokers talk to clients and to each other. Technical elves spend their days researching the thoughts the brokers ought to have. Journalists spend their careers reporting the talk on Wall Street, elvish or human. Their reports nourish in turn the talk among stockbrokers, between stockbrokers and their clients, and among the clients themselves. Wall Street buzzes with chatter and is littered with paper reporting the chatter.

A quarter of a century later, Jerry Antioch, a manager in the tax division of the Australian Treasury and an admirer of McCloskey and Klamer's work, ran the numbers again, and suggested that persuasion now represented even more (29%) of economic activity. Following the growth of social media – and the vastly more complex communications that occur between businesses and customers (and between businesses and businesses) as a result – we could safely argue that the figure continues to rise.

The better we are at persuading other people to do what we want – and indeed, when and how we want it – the more successful we'll become and the easier our lives will be. How can we get better at persuading people to do things? By understanding that the default method most of us use to persuade people to do things – giving them rational reasons, building a logical argument – is *not* the most effective way. In fact, it's deeply flawed.

Logic is not the best way to persuade people to do what you want

Many of us believe that the most effective way to persuade somebody to do something is to give them a reason why they should do it. Or a whole list of reasons why they should do it. This seems so stunningly obvious that many people never question it.

Actually, that last paragraph is not strictly true. If you are the boss or have superior status or power in a specific situation, then you know that sheer coercion can be the most effective way to persuade somebody to do something: "Do it because I told you to."

However, in many cases we are not the most important person in the scenario. And, in many cultures and many organisations, such aggressive power-based management and leadership techniques are either dead or dying out. Even in those more formal and hierarchical organisations where power is still wielded in such an unnuanced way, everybody knows deep down that this is not an ideal approach because although coercion may achieve short-term compliance, it builds up a great deal of resistance over the long term.

So, most of us rely on logical argument as our main tool of persuasion. "I would like you to do something and here is a very good reason why you should do it (and if that doesn't convince you I can come up with some more reasons)."

The problem is that building a logical argument is not the best way to persuade anyone to do anything. Often, it simply doesn't work.

Have you ever seen anyone at work make a decision that didn't seem to make any sense at all? Of course you have. We all have. Frequently.

Has anyone ever refused to do something that you wanted them to do even though all the logic in the world – the data, the case histories, the customer feedback, the client testimonials – proved that it was the right thing to do? Of course they have. It happens all the time.

The logical argument approach often fails miserably, and in these cases storytelling can be much more effective. That's because building a logical argument pushes people away from us, whereas storytelling draws them closer.

Building a logical argument encourages your audience to disagree with you

Essentially, when we try to use a logical argument to persuade someone, they immediately go on the defensive.

These defences take several forms. First, you are inevitably choosing *your* words to construct your logical argument and everyone that you talk to or write for will apply their own meaning to those words. It might sound odd, but words have very different meanings for different people.

Imagine you are selling a new product to a prospect. You're sure that they should adopt your idea because it's a new and exciting innovation that will revolutionise their business. And you find it very exciting – so exciting that you add several good reasons *why* it's so exciting.

However, the person you're talking to has just come out of a meeting with their boss where they have been criticised for a mistake they made last week, been told that the company doesn't like risk-takers, and warned that their next major mistake might be their last. Every time you introduce another feature in your product and explain that it is based on technology that is new, innovative, exciting, ahead of the curve or game-changing they aren't hearing "new", "innovative", "exciting", "ahead of the curve" or "game-changing"; they hear "untried", "untested", "very risky", "a really foolhardy option" and "potentially career-ending".

The more persuasive you become, the less they are persuaded. The more logical reasons you give to support your argument, the more reasons they are hearing to have nothing to do with you or your stupid and incredibly dangerous idea.

In this kind of scenario, there is nothing "wrong" with your argument, and the prospect doesn't even disagree with you, doesn't even have any counter-arguments. And yet your own argument effectively destroys itself.

This may be an extreme example, but the same principle holds true in every conversation you have. The words you use do not have the same meaning or emotional impact for your audience as they do for you; and in some instances, their meaning might be the exact opposite of what you expect it to be.

Worse still, even if your audience doesn't disagree with you, the fact that you have begun to try to steer them towards a particular direction will make them want to disagree with you. This phenomenon – which undermines the strength of any argument, however logical – was first codified by the American psychologist Jack Brehm.[2] It's called "psychological reactance". At its heart, it is the motivation to regain your freedom after it has been lost, or to defend your freedom when it seems to be threatened.

When somebody else attempts to persuade us to do something, we perceive this as a threat to our freedom. We believe we have a certain number of options, and when somebody tries to steer us towards one option, we sense that they are taking away our freedom to pursue the other options, and we don't like this – so we work to stop it happening.

When somebody pushes us in one direction, we push back.

This reactance is extremely powerful, and as the persuasive messages become more forceful and more controlling, the reactance gets stronger. What this means, ironically, is that the surer someone is of their arguments, the more powerful they think their logical reasons are, the more enthusiastically they communicate them, the more powerful is the reactance that they're creating.

Every time they land one of their killer points in their brilliantly argued presentation, they are strengthening the defences of their audience and increasing the chances that they will not agree.

A cursory glimpse at social media will show you this phenomenon in action.

Admittedly, the extremists ranting on social media may not be the same kind of people you will encounter in a work meeting. But the same basic principles hold true: the more logical reasons you give for your plan, the more logical reasons your audience will think up for themselves in favour of a plan B; the more fervently you argue for change, the more entrenched they will become in the belief that things should be left as they are.

It's tempting to believe that when you find yourself

presenting to, or debating with, more intelligent people, they will be able to open themselves up to your view. However, the evidence suggests that the more intelligent people are, the harder it is to persuade them to change their mind.

Smart people are simply *better* at psychological reactance. They find it easier to come up with counter arguments. They are more likely to be aware of data that suggests the opposite. They are more able to fashion a clever response quickly.

So how do you overcome psychological reactance? How do you get round people's defences? You won't be surprised to find that the answer is storytelling. Because storytelling takes things beyond logic and into the world of emotions.

Storytelling gives you access not just to people's thinking brain but also to their hearts

Oxytocin is sometimes referred to as "the cuddle hormone". It's a neurochemical that is released when we are shown trust or kindness or love. It's a signal that we are safe and that it is safe to approach and be with others. It motivates cooperation and increases our sense of empathy.

Oxytocin is released into the bloodstream during social bonding, during sexual activity, in the period after childbirth, and as mothers and babies bond when feeding. That should give you some idea how powerful it is, and what a positive feeling it generates. Oxytocin is also released into the bloodstream when we listen to or read a story.

Storytelling, then, is a direct way to make an audience more open, receptive, trusting and welcoming.

Why should storytelling create such a strong, positive feeling in us? Arguably, it has something to do with our origins – our beginnings both as individuals and as a species. For each of us, stories will have played a vital role in our lives. Not everybody has a happy childhood, of course, but for the majority, listening to stories evokes memories of a time in early childhood when we were being loved, cared for and entertained all at the same time – an important moment of bonding with parents or other carers.

Now, contrast that safe, warm, loved and loving moment with the times during early childhood when you were given logical reasons why you should do something. What were *they* like?

Almost invariably, the times when, as a child, you were given logical reasons why you should do something were the times when you were being asked (and, sooner or later, *told)* to do something that you did not want to do.

Why else were you being given *reasons* to do it? If a parent or carer was suggesting that you might like an ice cream or to watch your favourite TV show or a trip to the park to play in the playground, they are very unlikely to have given you a list of reasons why you would want to do it.

It's only when parents are trying to persuade children to do something against their will that the reasons and arguments come into play; when, for example, a visit is planned to family member that the child doesn't like. That's when the "But they've got such a lovely big garden for you to play in" or "Maybe Aunt Sarah will have that chocolate cake again" or "Look, if you just behave while you're there, you can stay up late tonight" logical arguments are aired.

In other words, we all learn when we are very young that if somebody gives us reasons why we should do something, it is because we *do not want to do it*. When somebody gives us a list of logical reasons to do something, it is because it will benefit *them* but not *us*.

Think very carefully about that next time you plan to unleash a list of logical reasons in a PowerPoint presentation. You are unleashing a deeply ingrained response in your audience that they do not want to do whatever it is you are proposing; and you are summoning memories of arguments and fights.

How is that going to help?

One of the primary reasons why storytelling can be more effective than building a logical argument is that it draws your audience towards you, rather than pushing them away. It resonates with fondly held memories, rather than unpleasant ones.

It's also more closely connected to how people make decisions.

To be persuasive, you need to align with your audience's decision-making process

When you communicate at work, and you naturally want your communications to be effective, it's not enough simply to push content out into the world. It's also important to think about how readers read, how audiences listen and, crucially, how people make decisions.

If you are trying to influence other people's decisions, you must take account of how those decisions are made. When you use storytelling, you can align your communication to your audience's decision-making process more closely than you can when basing your communication solely on logical arguments.

This is because people don't make decisions based on logic. They make decisions based on their emotional response. To persuade, influence, inspire or change people, you must make an emotional connection – and storytelling is a very effective way of doing that.

You may well feel the need to argue with that previous paragraph. What's all this about people making decisions based on emotions? Maybe *some* people do, but you don't. You're a smart, rational, analytical thinker; you study the data carefully and you make decisions for the right reasons.

The neuroscience, however, suggests otherwise. Although most of us *think* we make decisions for good, solid, rational, logical reasons, in fact that's not what happens. We make decisions based on our emotions and then, having made the decision, we look around for a logical argument to back up our decision. When we explain our decision to others, or even justify our decision to ourselves, we reach for (and find) some logical reasons, but they are not what prompted the decision in the first instance.

Let me be very clear. I am not suggesting that emotions merely *influence* our decisions. I'm saying something more extreme than that. I'm saying that without emotions we cannot make decisions.

This is a relatively recent discovery, not widely known or understood, and deeply counterintuitive to those who have been raised to believe that emotions get in the way of good decision-making. In many organisations, where the admonition to "keep emotions out of it" can still be heard, this remains the conventional thinking.

Keeping emotions out of it is not only a bad idea, it's impossible.

The neuroscientist Antonio Damásio has written extensively on this subject following research conducted with a patient he refers to as "Elliot".[3] It is in the nature of neuroscientific research that much of our learning comes from studying the behaviour of people whose brains have been damaged in some way. The emotional centre in Elliot's brain was damaged so that he lost the ability to feel emotions. However, his IQ remained the same and he was perfectly capable of understanding and making logical, rational arguments. He could draw up a list of pros and cons, arguments for and against, as well as anyone.

He could think about a decision. He could put together all the evidence. But he couldn't *make* a decision. Faced with overwhelming evidence that a particular decision was the right one, he still couldn't choose it because, without emotions, it turns out, there is nothing to guide a human being to a decision, even when it is logically obvious.

How do we know when a decision is the right one? It has to *feel* right.

Elliot's case suggests that all the logic in the world won't make us choose A over B, if A doesn't *feel* like the right answer.

Although Elliot offers the most graphic example of how emotions are the vital first step in decision-making – the catalyst without which the decision-making process cannot happen – other studies have indicated clearly that it is our emotions that guide our decisions, not our logical mind.

The Iowa gambling task[4] was constructed by Antoine Bechara, then assistant professor of neurology at the University of Iowa College of Medicine, along with Antonio Damásio and other colleagues. The research subjects were given four decks of cards and were able to win or lose money (from an imaginary budget) by simply drawing cards. However, the decks had been carefully prepared so that drawing from two of the decks led to consistent small wins with few penalties, whereas the other two decks had occasional high payouts but also long periods of losses (which outweighed the gains). The logical choice over the long term was to stick to the two "safe" decks with the consistent small wins and avoid the other two more erratic and "dangerous" decks.

Usually, after drawing about fifty cards, most subjects focused increasingly on the two safe decks. So, had they worked out what was going on? Not exactly. In fact, it wasn't until around the eightieth card that most people could explain what was going on, and why they were now sticking mainly to just two of the four decks. This was the point at which they understood logically what was happening.

But the real insight into how we make decisions came from a variation of the research. In some of the studies, subjects were hooked up to a device that measured their galvanic skin response, which showed that they typically had a stress reaction as they reached towards the "dangerous" decks after only about ten cards.

So the emotion that triggered the decision to avoid the decks began to kick in after ten cards. It took them until fifty cards to respond to the emotional signals and make the decision, and then a further thirty cards before they understood the logical "reasons" why they had made the decision. I've put "reasons" in quotation marks because, of course, if someone can't construct the logical basis for the decision until after they've made it, then it clearly *isn't* the basis for the decision. The decision to move away from the unsafe decks happens because they *feel* wrong, they provoke anxiety and stress; the reason why they feel wrong is only revealed to the decision-maker much later.

Do the logical factors contribute to the decision? Yes. But do they *drive* the decision? No. The emotions drive the decision.

If you want to reach people and persuade them to make a decision, you have to align with a fundamentally emotional decision-making process; you have to have an emotional conversation with them as well as a logical one.

Of course, we still need the logical argument as well as the emotional factors because people like to have logical arguments to explain their decisions. But these are essentially retrofitted after the decision has been made. Why is this so little known? Because our logical mind works hard to convince us that it is in charge – and has been in charge all along. (Right now, there's a good chance that your logical mind, alarmed that its supremacy might be under threat, is explaining to you that this is all nonsense.)

As the Iowa gambling task suggests, our logical, rational mind takes much longer than our emotional decision-making process. But once the logical mind has caught up, it rapidly claims responsibility for the decision.

Like a boss who only turns up for the final meeting on a project but who then assumes all the credit for the work of their team, our logical mind asserts itself as the prime mover in the decision. Our logical mind's desire to take the credit for whatever we decide to do is so strong that it does it even when it is provably false.

Michael Gazzaniga, professor of psychology at the University of California, Santa Barbara, showed how strong our desire is to give a reason for a decision, even when we don't *know* why the decision was made.[5] Building on work that he had undertaken as a graduate student with Nobel prize-winning neuropsychologist Roger Sperry, Gazzaniga carried out research with subjects in whom the left and right hemispheres of the brain were severed. This meant that when a picture was shown to a subject's right hemisphere, the left hemisphere wasn't able to articulate what the right hemisphere had seen.

In a typical example from the research, a snowy winter setting was shown to the right hemisphere and the subject was then asked to point to a card that represented what they had just seen. They pointed to a shovel, which was the correct answer. But when asked to explain why they had chosen the shovel, they could not refer to the snowy picture. Since the left hemisphere hadn't seen the card, they didn't "know" that they had seen it.

Did they just shrug and say "I don't know"? Not at all. In each case the subject's left-brain hemisphere came up with a reason. It was a perfectly sensible, rational reason why somebody might choose to point to a picture of a shovel – but it didn't have anything to do with just having seen the picture of the snowy scene.

In similar research, each subject's right hemisphere was given the message that they should go to a water fountain outside the room and get a drink. When the subjects stood up and headed for the door, they were asked, "Where are you going?" The left hemisphere did not know anything about the water fountain and did not know it was going to get a drink. But, again, the subjects didn't just say "I don't know". They worked on the basis that there must be a reason and so retrofitted a reason that seemed to make sense (all the time unaware that this was what they were doing). Their left hemisphere came up with a rational sensible reason. For example: "I'm going to get my coat because I'm cold."

Gazzaniga and his colleague Joseph Ledoux christened this brain function "the interpreter". The job of the interpreter is seemingly to come up with a logical reason where in fact there is none.

In his book, *Tales from Both Sides of the Brain*, Gazzaniga writes:

> The interpreter not only took note; it tried to make "sense" out of the behavior by keeping a running narrative going on about why a string of behaviors was occurring. It is a precious device and most likely uniquely human. It is working in us all the time as we try to explain why we like something or have a particular opinion, or rationalize something we have done. It is the interpreter device that takes the inputs from the massively modularized and automatic brain of ours and

creates order from chaos. It comes up with the "makes sense" explanation.

Gazzaniga concludes: "Nice try, interpreter!"

While we are only at the beginning of truly understanding how the brain works, and certainly can't claim to know exactly how decisions are made, research like this offers the valuable insight that people like to make their decisions seem rational, even when they're not, and will offer a logical reason for their behaviour – absolutely convinced that it's true – even when it's demonstrably not.

When someone gives you feedback to explain why they didn't agree with your proposal, the reasons they give may possibly be partly true, but they are also likely to contain retrofitted post-rationalisations for a decision that was made based on emotions.

If you're the boss or a successful entrepreneur you can probably get away with saying "It just doesn't feel right" on occasion, but the rest of us will tend to think that we need to supply logical reasons to back up our decisions, and so the interpreter springs into action on our behalf.

So, to communicate effectively with someone, we must make what we say *feel* right, rather than merely make sense.

As well as being more involving, and better aligned with our real decision-making process than logical arguments, storytelling has another great advantage. If you try to persuade somebody by giving them a bunch of reasons, they will tend to quickly forget the reasons. If you use storytelling, they will remember much more of what you said.

Stories are more memorable

We know that stories are more memorable than facts, but there is some debate about exactly how much more memorable. A Google search will reveal repeated claims that stories are 22 times more memorable – an extraordinary difference, but this turns out to be one of those "internet facts" that is hard to substantiate. It is usually attributed to the cognitive psychologist Jerome Bruner, but a study of his books reveals that he never actually said it. What Bruner did say is this:

> Perhaps the most basic thing that can be said about human memory after a century of intensive research is that unless a detail is placed into a structured pattern, it is rapidly forgotten.[6]

Bruner describes human beings as "storytelling creatures" and concludes from his extensive research that human beings have "a readiness or predisposition to organise experience into a narrative form, into plot structures". So, if we can place our communication into a storytelling or narrative form, it is more easily assimilated.

Bruner doesn't put a number on this, but others have tried to do so. In a 1969 study at Stanford, students were tested on their ability to remember twelve words. Half of the group were simply told to remember the words; the other half were told that their task was to place the twelve words into a story which they would make up themselves – and to remember the words in this way

Of the students who created a story, 93% were later able to remember all the words, whereas only 13% of those who were tasked with simply remembering the list could do so. This suggests that stories may be seven times more memorable than facts alone. It's not 22 times, but it is a significant difference.

In their book *Made to Stick*, brothers Chip and Dan Heath recount a study which they undertook with students (also at Stanford) on a similar theme, but more structured, and more akin to a business setting in that the facts were delivered in presentations.[7] After a gap of only ten minutes, only 5% of the audience could recall any individual statistics from the standard presentations; but two thirds of the audience could remember similar details from those presentations which were in the form of a story. In this case, we might suggest that stories proved twelve times as memorable as statistics.

If you were asked to go to the supermarket and buy twelve grocery items, you would need to write them down or you would forget some. However, if you were going to the supermarket to buy twelve items to make a favourite recipe, you would have no trouble remembering them: the recipe creates the narrative structure – first this and then some of that – which will make the individual items stick in your memory.

Traditional show-business memory acts use this kind of approach. Comedian Nick Mohammed both genuinely uses this technique and spoofs it. He really does have the ability to remember every card in a pack of 52 cards in sequence after scanning the pack for a few seconds, but also in his comedy character, Mr Swallow, he spoofs the memory technique by creating the most outrageous storytelling links between different words. Finally, Mr Swallow admits that the real problem is remembering the *first* word in the list, because there is nothing to link it to. How does he do it? "By brute force!" is Mr Swallow's shouted explanation – the comedy reflecting the truth of just how hard it is for us to remember anything without the aid of a narrative structure.

After you spend hours creating a PowerPoint presentation filled with wonderfully relevant logical arguments, compelling facts and unarguable data, then spend more time rehearsing, and finally give your vital presentation to the board, the first reason why they won't approve your idea is that they simply won't remember what you said. Ten minutes later they will not recall your arguments, facts and data – however compelling.

Unless you wrap them up in a story structure.

Why is a story so much more memorable? The neuroscience suggests that it is because when we listen to a bunch of facts only a limited amount of our brain gets activated; basically, only the language-processing parts. Just enough to decode the meaning but nothing else. But when we listen to a story, many other areas in our brain light up – the areas that we would use if we were experiencing the events of the story. As the speaker tells the story, we effectively live the story. As cognitive psychologist Roger Shank puts it: "Humans are not ideally set up to understand logic; they are ideally set up to understand stories."

Just as storytelling played a vital role at the beginning of most of our lives, it seems likely that it played a vital role in the dawn of our species: that storytelling was a means of passing on valuable, perhaps life-saving, information from one individual to another. Stories were a way to use language to condense key learnings into an easily understood form. Robert McKee, the Hollywood screenwriting guru, puts it like this:

> Stories are equipment for living. Our appetite for story is a reflection of the profound human need to grasp the patterns of living.

This may also explain why stories tend to follow the problem/resolution structure that we will meet in the next chapter.

While it's intriguing to speculate on exactly *why* storytelling resonates so powerfully with us, for now it matters only that storytelling *does* have this extraordinary effect and that we can harness this power in our communications. But before we can do that, we need to be clear on exactly what a story is.

2

What is a story?

Understanding what a story is, and how it works; and why, before we do anything else, we need to save a cat

When Paulie arrives, Chris is sitting on the sofa, staring disconsolately at his laptop.

Paulie was expecting Chris to be dressed up and ready for a night out on the town. Instead, Chris sits there, still in his underwear. The floor of his apartment is strewn with discarded rubbish and dirty laundry.

When Paulie asks what the matter is, Chris explains that he is struggling to write a screenplay. As he talks, his moaning about writer's block and his inability to find his character's arc morphs into existential dread about the fact that he can't find his own. "Says in these film-writing books that every character has an arc. Understand? Like, everybody starts out somewhere. Then they do something, or something gets done to them. Changes their life. That's called their arc. Where's my arc?"

Paulie is quick to soothe Chris's worries by pointing out that he doesn't have an arc either. "I was born, grew up, spent a few years in the army, a few more in the can ... and here I am – a half a wise guy."

Paulie is (in this moment, anyway) considerably more

than half of a wise guy. He is very wise indeed, because he understands that not everything in life is a story.

Admittedly this is all a scene from Series 2 of *The Sopranos*, so in one sense they are both characters with a clear arc given to them by the show's creators. But within the show's own reality, Paulie has happened upon an important truth: most things in real life aren't stories.

In understanding this, he reveals himself to be far cleverer than many of today's major companies, and certainly their marketing departments – who act as though *everything* is a story. On social media I encountered a photo of some packaging from Jeni's, an ice cream company based in Columbus, Ohio, which announced proudly: "We make ice cream that tells stories of the people, places and cultures that inspire us." The photo was gaining quite a bit of traction on social media, but not in a good way.

"Imagine writing this down!" wrote one person. "If my tub of ice cream started telling stories I'd kill it with a hammer," wrote another. A third added perceptively: "You could replace 'ice cream' in that sentence with pretty much any product or brand these days."

Let's state a simple fact before we go any further: Jeni's does not make ice cream that tells stories of the people, places and cultures that inspire them because ice cream doesn't tell stories.

As another comment noted: "This whole idea of stories is getting out of hand."

It certainly is. "Every feed has a story to tell," suggests a recent TV ad for Aptamil follow-on milk. Really? What story would that be? Aptamil tells us. "The way you feed your baby tells *your* story," the ad continues.

The way you feed your baby may say quite a lot about

your present circumstances or state of mind: anywhere on a spectrum from chronically sleep-deprived, anxious, stressed and full of self-doubt through to calm, relaxed, blissful and, as some other copywriter would probably tell us, "being the best you that you can be".

But that's not a *story*.

In my consultancy work I regularly encounter companies who tell me proudly that they are storytellers or claim that their brands or products tell stories. However, when I challenge them to tell me one of these stories, there is usually an embarrassed silence. Nobody knows what these supposed stories actually are. For the very good reason that there *are* no stories.

The words "story" and "storytelling" have become like "passionate", "strategic", "customer-centric", "bespoke" (and story's close friend "journey") – buzzwords that every company or brand tries to drop into its messaging somewhere, usually without giving any thought to their meaning.

Our individual experiences with these companies tend to demonstrate that many of the people who work for them are neither "passionate" nor "customer-centric"; and our experience of the badly targeted messages they send us, the menu and sub-menus we wade through when we call them or the scripted messages of their chatbot reveals that there is little about them that is "bespoke". Companies persist in telling us that our call is important to them but the fact that we are in a queue makes it clear to us that it isn't. Companies, we must conclude, like to use words that sound good even when they don't mean them. And, when we deal with companies, we rarely encounter any stories.

There is sometimes *one* story. Many brands have replaced the "about us" section of their website with an "our story" section, and this sometimes really does tell a story – the origin story of the company's founder and their struggles to create the product or service.

But in most cases the word "story" is used randomly and incorrectly. Somebody somewhere has decided that storytelling is a good thing. And so they throw in the word "story" wherever it seems to fit.

Rather than having any benefit for the company this misuse of story simply annoys customers, as the comments about Jeni's demonstrate.

If you want to use story as more than a buzzword – if you want to harness the power of storytelling – then you need to know what so many companies evidently don't know. You need to know what a story actually is.

This chapter explores some of the most important and helpful definitions and descriptions of story, summarising the work of those who have helped to delineate a story's key elements. In this way we can build up a clearer picture of what makes a story – and, more importantly, what makes a *good* story.

A beginning, a middle and an end ... oh, and an obstacle

One of the most cited descriptions of a story is the idea that it has a beginning, a middle and an end. This is helpful but not *that* helpful. After all, so does a three-course meal, a motorway and a typical working day. We clearly need to know slightly more than this.

The idea originates in Aristotle's *Poetics*, which contains the influential Greek philosopher's thoughts on drama. By "a beginning" Aristotle meant an event that leads naturally to a further event, but which is itself not directly caused by a previous event. By "an ending" he meant the opposite: an event caused by a previous event, but not naturally leading onto further events. The "middle" contains a series of events that are causally linked.

A story, then, is self-contained. It should be very clear where it starts, and equally clear where it stops. And each event in the story should follow on naturally from the previous one.

Elsewhere in Aristotle's works, in *Rhetoric*, he introduced the idea of the three unities, which can be summarised like this:

- unity of action: a drama should have one principal action
- unity of time: the action should occur over a period of no more than 24 hours
- unity of place: the action should happen in one location.

These have been interpreted and reinterpreted many times since, by critics and authors in Renaissance Italy through to the contemporary American playwright David Mamet.[1]

Critics have often argued with the concept of the unity of time and the unity of place, considering them unnecessary restrictions (although, as the TV series 24 illustrated, preserving unity of time can add urgency and excitement to a drama).

It's the idea of unity of action that has remained a clear and valuable guideline to storytellers through to today. In Mamet's words, the unity of action says, "in effect, that the play should be about one thing. And that thing should be what the hero is trying to get. Unstinting application of this rule makes great plays."

Here Mamet has introduced a second idea: that somebody is trying to get something. The essence of drama or story is "the quest of the hero to overcome those things which prevent him from achieving a specific, acute goal".

This in turn illuminates the three-act structure of traditional drama that is implied by Aristotle's beginning, middle and end. In Act One we see the hero's everyday life, leading up to the moment when the quest first becomes obvious; Act Two shows the hero trying to overcome everything that gets in their way as they pursue their quest; Act Three contains the resolution when the quest is finally achieved.

All this talk of heroes and quests makes it sound as though stories only exist in a world of *Lord of the Rings* or *Game of Thrones*. But anybody in any setting can be a hero, and the quest can range from fighting terrorists, to marrying the person of your dreams, to making your way home to Kansas. It can be about destroying a ring, escaping from prison, finding true romance, or finding a fish. It can be motivated by a desperate desire to change your world, or a desire to keep things exactly as they are in the face of potential disruption.

The Pulitzer Prize-winning writer Robert Olen Butler expressed the idea like this:

Story is a yearning meeting an obstacle.

The same idea was expressed as an equation by the American literary scholar Jonathan Gottschall in *The Storytelling Animal: How Stories Make Us Human*:

Story = Character ɪ Predicament + Attempted extrication

The key idea is that a story must have a problem and an attempted solution. A story without this emotional arc isn't really a story. It's just an anecdote.

For thousands of years this has been intuitively understood. Now we have the science to back it up, thanks to research by MIT's Laboratory for Social Machines and McKinsey's consumer tech and media team, who developed machine-learning models to "watch" video footage (including films and TV shows) and track their positive or negative emotional content second by second. These sophisticated models tracked plot, characters, dialogue, camera angles and music to determine the story's emotional arc.

After studying thousands of videos, the research concluded that stories with a strong problem/solution emotional arc were most popular with audiences, generating more likes and better engagement metrics.

This fundamental emotional arc has been expressed in many different ways over the years. The screenwriters Ben Hecht and Charles MacArthur were so successful in Hollywood in the 1930s that a film was made about them. *Boy Meets Girl* is a screwball comedy starring James Cagney and Pat O'Brien as two screenwriters, Law and Benson, who are based closely on Hecht and MacArthur. In one scene they are pitching a film idea to a studio boss, brilliantly improvising the script for a romantic comedy from items they find in his office. At the end of their manic pitch, in triumphant conclusion, they sum up the whole plot:

> *Law:* Boy meets girl.
> *Benson:* Boy loses girl.
> *Law:* Boy gets girl.

... and the studio boss is sold on the idea.

This snappy pitch adheres to the three-act structure, giving us a clear beginning, middle and end, and also underlines that a story requires jeopardy ("boy loses girl") to interest an audience.

Questions, questions, questions

Another way of expressing this fundamental idea was mooted by Bernard Grebanier, who believed that every plot could be expressed in terms of an overriding question.[2] Grebanier's Proposition, as it is known, is the fundamental question that drives the plot. In Law and Benson's mythical pitch, the proposition would be: "*Will* boy get girl?" Grebanier stated that any good story could be expressed in this way: will Romeo and Juliet find happiness together? Will Marlin find Nemo? Can John McClane possibly defeat the terrorists?

It is the uncertainty behind this question that keeps the audience engaged. Will the hero achieve their quest? Will the couple end up together? Will the good guys defeat the bad guys? Will the Universe be saved from ultimate destruction?

In some genres the structure can be understood as a *series* of questions. Books that become known as "page-turners" keep the reader turning those pages by posing or implying a series of questions. Is this guy everything he seems to be? Will this woman listen to the wise advice of her best friend? All right, she didn't, but who is that in the van that keeps following them? Surely, they're not going to be stupid enough to wander off into that dark forest? Okay they did, but surely they're not going to be stupid enough to split up? Okay, so they have, but which one of them will that shadowy figure chase? And so on ...

The hero with a thousand faces ... and how *Star Wars* very nearly never happened

In the mid-1970s George Lucas was one of the hottest young directors in Hollywood. His 1973 film *American Graffiti*, a homage to the early days of youth culture, had been a commercial smash (and remains one of the most profitable films ever made). He therefore believed that he had the clout to do whatever he wanted for his next project – and what he wanted to do was make a science fiction film.

But to get a sci-fi film made, Lucas faced three obstacles.

First, science fiction was a deeply unfashionable genre in Hollywood. Second, as if to underline that, Lucas's debut film *THX 1138* was a dystopian science fiction film and was a flop, so there was always going to be a mountain to climb persuading anyone to finance another sci-fi outing.

Perhaps Lucas's career momentum could get him over those two obstacles, but it couldn't help him deal with the third: the fact that he simply couldn't finish the screenplay. He wrote draft after draft, but the results he came up with pleased neither himself nor the peer group of fellow directors that he shared his early drafts with for their feedback. Over a period of many months, the project seemed to be going nowhere. And then Lucas started reading a book by Joseph Campbell.

Born in 1904, Campbell entered young adulthood brimming with potential; he combined academic achievement with sporting prowess. For a time, he was among the fastest half-mile runners in the world, and he followed a master's degree in mediaeval literature with continued study in Europe, in both France and Germany. During his European travels, he was introduced to modern European literature (notably, the work of James Joyce), he learned Sanskrit (giving him access to ancient scriptures) and had a random meeting with Indian philosopher Jiddu Krishnamurti, which influenced him profoundly.

Campbell's return to the United States coincided with the Great Depression. Unable to find employment, the promising start to his career came to a grinding halt and Campbell lived for five years in a rented shack in Woodstock, New York.

During this enforced hiatus, Campbell read for up to nine hours a day. And as he read widely – exploring the folklore and mythology of different cultures and eras – he began to notice the strong similarities that kept emerging. Remarkably, the same basic structural pattern occurred in the myths and stories of cultures from around the world and through the ages.

Campbell began to develop the idea that, borrowing a term from his hero Joyce, he would call the monomyth: that in any culture's mythology there "will always be the one, shape-shifting yet marvellously constant story that we find".

In essence, Campbell said that there is one fundamental story idea that underpins all other stories, although he allowed himself that qualifying adjective "shape-shifting" to concede that the story shows itself in varying ways. It was this idea, explored at length by Campbell in *The Hero with a Thousand Faces*, that intrigued and inspired George Lucas.[3]

After reading Campbell's ideas, Lucas quickly reshaped his *Star Wars* script in a way which overtly mirrored the pattern that Campbell had called "the hero's journey". Having done so, Lucas was able to finish the script, to pitch the film successfully and to create a film that launched one of the most lucrative and culturally important franchises and one of the most powerful stories of the modern era.

Here is how Campbell defines the hero's journey, at its simplest:

> A hero ventures forth from the world of common day into a region of supernatural wonder: fabulous forces are there encountered and a decisive victory is won: the hero comes back from this mysterious adventure with the power to bestow boons on his fellow man.

Campbell's work has been criticised by other academics for oversimplification and for selecting the source material that backs up his idea of the monomyth while ignoring stories that diverge from it. Even if these criticisms are true, even if Campbell did slightly over-claim, he clearly identified a story that can be found across times and across cultures with remarkable consistency and regularity. He showed – and the success of *Star Wars* underlined – that there are certain themes which when rendered in story form seem to appeal to huge numbers of people around the world.

Campbell's theory and the success of *Star Wars* not only reflect how stories have always underpinned ancient mythology; they have also helped to shape the way stories are right now. In the years before *Star Wars*, Hollywood had been going through an experimental period, during which a young new wave of directors (Martin Scorsese, Robert Altman, Francis Ford Coppola and others) had been trying to escape from conventional story forms believing they could reshape the entire industry more in line with the work of the European avant-garde film directors that they admired (Louis Malle, Claude Chabrol, François Truffaut, Alain Resnais and Jean-Luc Godard). The mixed commercial results of their works coupled with the staggering success of *Star Wars* effectively ended that idea. Clearly audiences still preferred conventional stories, and as a result of this Hollywood Studios tried to emulate the approach of *Star Wars*.

The hero's journey ... made simple

Once the industry realised that the film followed a specific template they became extremely interested in understanding and copying it. However, Campbell's work, although fascinating, is not an easy read. It has its own jargon, jumps quickly from subject to subject, and the writing style is quite florid. Campbell divides the hero's journey into a complex 17-stage structure and goes deeply into religious and spiritual areas that the casual reader can easily get lost in.

A key turning point for the industry was when Christopher

Vogler, a young script analyst at Disney, converted the book into an accessible seven-page summary, *A Practical Guide to The Hero with a Thousand Faces*. This quickly became the formula for success in films; and Vogler later developed it into his book, *The Writer's Journey: Mythic Structure for Writers*.[4]

The essence of the structure is this:

The story begins in the hero's ordinary world. The hero receives a call to adventure. At first the hero resists but they are then encouraged by a mentor to take the first step. As they pursue the adventure, they encounter a series of increasingly difficult challenges but also meet helpers. Faced with a supreme challenge they have moments of doubt, but with knowledge from their mentor and/or assistance from their helpers, they finally gain their reward and return to the ordinary world, usually being pursued and facing further risks. They return to the ordinary world with some kind of gift, treasure, boon or wisdom that will benefit the world.

This structure is closely followed in the story of *Star Wars*:

The story begins in the hero's (*Luke's*) ordinary world. The hero receives a call to adventure (*Princess Leia's message*). At first the hero resists but they are then encouraged by a mentor (*Obi-Wan*) to take the first step. As they pursue the adventure, they encounter a series of increasingly difficult challenges (*mastering the lightsabre/getting trapped in the trash compactor/ various battles*) but also meet helpers (*Han Solo/Chewbacca*). Faced with a supreme challenge they have moments of doubt (*being tempted to the Dark Side*), but with knowledge from their mentor and/or assistance from their helpers, they finally gain their reward and return to the ordinary world, usually being pursued and facing further risks. They return to the ordinary world with some kind of gift, treasure, boon or wisdom that will benefit the world (*destruction of the Death Star*).

As soon as you are aware of this structure you will start to see it again and again in films, TV dramas, plays and novels. And even when stories fail to follow the structure faithfully, you will usually see many of the elements of it employed.

Once upon a time there was ...

Causality, as has been noted, is essential to storytelling, and this idea has been elegantly expressed by Kenn Adams, the artistic director of Synergy Theatre in San Francisco. Adams developed what he termed the "story spine" as a structure to help actors create long-form improvisations. He outlined the approach and his wider ideas in his book *How to Improvise a Full-Length Play: The Art of Spontaneous Theatre*, but in fact his ideas have transcended the relatively niche world of improv to become pivotal in many of the biggest-grossing films of our era.

The story spine looks like this:

Once upon a time ...
Every day ...
But then one day ...
Because of that ...
Because of that ...
Because of that ....
Until finally ...

This simple formula became instantly more famous when Pixar story artist Emma Coates tweeted what she called the company's *22 Rules of Storytelling* and the story spine was right there at number four.

In fact, the other 21 rules are mostly advice for writers on the *process* of writing and the *job* of being a writer. For example: "Come up with your ending before you figure out your middle. Seriously. Endings are hard, get yours working up front." The story spine is the only rule on that list that is unambiguously a rule of storytelling; it's not telling you how to write, it's telling you what a story needs to be. And you can see quite easily how closely Pixar's successful films have followed it. Here's *Finding Nemo*:

- Once upon a time there was a fish called Marlin.
- Every day, he warned his son Nemo that the ocean was a dangerous place.
- Until one day Nemo ignored his father's wise words and swam away.
- Because of that, he was captured and found himself in a fish tank.
- Because of that Marlin set off to rescue Nemo.
- Until finally he found Nemo.

On the surface, Pixar's *Inside Out* seems like a very different film. But dig a little deeper, and you'll find that it follows the same structure:

- Once upon a time there was a girl called Riley.
- Every day her actions were controlled by Joy who ran her emotions and tried to keep Sadness fully under control.
- Until one day, when Riley moved to a new city, her sad feelings burst through.
- Because of that Joy tried to make things better by eliminating sad memories but in fact that just made everything worse.

- Because of that Joy and Sadness had to find a way to collaborate.
- Until finally Joy realised that every emotion including sadness is important and should be felt.

The idea of causality was succinctly summarised by Aline Brosh McKenna, who wrote the script of *The Devil Wears Prada*. "You want all your scenes to have a 'because' between them and not an 'and then' between them. ... When you're writing a script, you don't want to feel like these things could be in any order. And if they can, then that's a problem."

Why do stories follow the same pattern?

If the stories that become the most popular tend to follow a particular pattern, why should this be? What is it about this particular problem/solution story shape that makes it perennially successful?

Most of the theories that have been put forward to answer this question revolve around the idea of stories as some kind of rehearsal of real life. Some suggest that stories show us a series of problems of the kind that we are likely to face and provide solutions that we can borrow. In effect we use stories in the way a pilot uses a flight simulator: stories are obviously not real life, and yet they help us learn certain key skills that we will need in real life, without the dangers we would face if we had to pick up these skills while facing genuine jeopardy.

However, the idea that stories offer quite such a clear tutorial seems a little unlikely given the extreme and exaggerated nature of many plots. Few of us have to save the universe, defuse ticking bombs, reveal murderers or deal with a bunch of pesky reanimated dinosaurs on a regular basis.

Other theories suggest, perhaps more believably, that

although stories don't give us specific solutions that we can use in our own lives, they do reveal to us the basic patterns of our lives – the *kind* of journey that we will all go on. They help us to make sense of our lives by making the shape of real life a bit more obvious.

Yet other theories suggest that stories aren't there to *prepare* us for the struggles of real life but are more of a post-struggle catharsis. No, we're not fighting the battles we see on screen, but we do fight battles in our lives every day – the struggle to pay the bills, the hard work needed to maintain relationships, an individual's fight with physical or mental health issues – and the battles we see on screen give us an easy way to access and process the emotions about our own battles that we may suppress in everyday life.

Stories also play a role in reminding us all that we have agency: that we can take responsibility and make things happen. Perhaps no one will ever call us a hero, perhaps we will never really feel like one, but there are times in life when we can play a central role, face up to challenges and help those around us.

The story so far

So, to summarise, what are the key elements of a story?

A good story must:

- have a well-defined beginning, middle and end
- be about one thing
- have a clearly understood quest (which can also be expressed as a question)
- follow a problem/solution structure on the way to achieve that quest
- be driven by a clear causal chain.

It follows that a story that starts randomly, meanders from subject to subject for no obvious reason, has a very flat emotional arc and no clear end point is a bad story.

There are, of course, exceptions. Some great novelists break all the rules and create remarkable literature, but this book is not written for the next Herman Melville, Virginia Woolf or Alice Walker. What's important, if you wish to employ storytelling at work, is that you understand the rules of conventional storytelling.

Up to now we've looked at the rules for what might be called the external story – the structure and plot. Equally important, but less immediately obvious, is what has to happen within the hero.

Under pressure, we learn

In parallel with the plot, alongside the visible structure of the story, there is also an internal structure and an important internal change.

During the hero's journey, the hero learns something.

One way of representing this is to say that the hero begins the story with a false view of the world that needs to be corrected. Alternatively, it could be said that the hero begins the story with the generally accepted view of the world – the received wisdom of their culture – and the journey they go on takes them beyond societal norms to learn a new truth.

In *Star Wars* Luke Skywalker learns about the Force. In *The Matrix* Neo learns that he is "the one". In *The Wizard of Oz*, Dorothy learns that she does not need the help of a wizard to get home.

In a sense, the challenges that the hero has to face seem to have been put there for a reason – to teach them what they needed to learn. Without being put under pressure, without being tested, the hero would never make the leap of understanding required to grasp the lesson.

Once they have been tested and come through the test successfully, the hero is a changed person – and this change is the true heart of the story. This is beautifully exemplified in the classic western *The Magnificent Seven* (itself a reworking of Akira Kurosawa's *The Seven Samurai*).

In the film, Chris is a mercenary – a gunman hired by the frightened inhabitants of a Mexican village to protect them from marauding bandits led by Calvera. Chris recruits six fellow gunmen and together they initially fight off Calvera. However, they then get overambitious and Calvera outwits them, taking their guns.

Wanting to avoid any unnecessary bloodshed which might bring the law down on his head, Calvera offers Chris a deal: he will spare them, and even give them their guns back if they agree to simply ride away and forget the villagers. Calvera knows they will take the deal because they are mercenaries. They don't care about the villagers. They were only there for the money.

The mercenaries leave, but Chris returns and shoots Calvera.

As Calvera lies bleeding on the ground he asks in astonishment: "You came back? To a place like this? Why? A man like you? Why?"

The answer, of course, is that Chris is no longer "a man like" he used to be. Under pressure he has learned a lesson and changed forever. He originally came for just the money, but now he has formed an emotional bond with the villagers.

So, having survived tremendous challenges, the hero learns something important about himself. It is a lesson that applies to everyone reading or watching the story.

The lesson that *Star Wars* and *The Wizard of Oz* teaches is that *we* have agency, *we* can take responsibility.

Their story, not your story

Understanding that the lesson is not just for the hero but also for the audience leads us to an idea encapsulated by the Nobel Prize-winning novelist John Steinbeck when he wrote: "If a story is not about the hearer, he will not listen."

Although the hero of the story may be a warrior for good in a dystopian future or a young girl from Depression-era Kansas in a psychedelic alternative reality, we – the hearers – have to see an aspect of ourselves in them, or at least see a reflection of our struggles in their struggle.

If a story is 100% about someone else, we don't care. In some sense, on some level, we have to feel that the story is about us. We are usually not conscious of this connection, but if it isn't there, we stop reading or stop watching.

This idea that we must see ourselves in the hero brings us to one of the most important techniques in modern storytelling: the intriguingly titled "Save the Cat".

The five-second difference between success and failure

The 1989 film *Planes, Trains and Automobiles* is a cult comedy classic – a very funny film with two great lead performances by John Candy and Steve Martin.

However, it was nearly a complete disaster.

In fact, it turns out that the difference between a comedy classic and a complete disaster comes down to just five seconds of screen time. Or, if you prefer, just thirteen words. The "Save the Cat" moment.

Planes Trains and Automobiles is about a comically mismatched pair. Steve Martin's character Neal is an ad executive trying to get home to Chicago for Thanksgiving.

He's faced with a series of obstacles that get in his way from an extreme blizzard to John Candy's Del, a shower-curtain-ring salesman, whose fortunes become inextricably linked with Neal's as they both try to continue their journeys. For most of the film, Neal would like to get rid of Del every bit as much as he would like to get back to Chicago (although he becomes more compassionate when he finally realises Del has nowhere to go on Thanksgiving).

Before it was released, the film was shown to a preview audience – standard Hollywood procedure to check the film against a typical film audience and allow the director to make a few final tweaks based on their feedback.

But in this case, it became instantly clear that there was something fundamentally wrong. Exactly what happened was recounted by the film's editor, Paul Hirsch, in his book *A Long Time Ago, in a Cutting Room Far, Far Away*:

> The preview was a disaster. After about 20 minutes, a couple of people walked out. Then a few more a few minutes later. I had never seen this before and my stomach sank. More people left. And then *a whole row* got up and left. I was shocked ...
>
> We worked like crazy and screened again. The results were better but only a little. We remixed and screened the picture twice a week for the rest of September. Nine previews in all.

Nine previews is *not* standard procedure. There was clearly a serious problem here. Eventually, the film's makers isolated exactly what it was that was making audiences walk out. The audience thought that Del was exploiting Neal, who ends up paying for everything – so they didn't like Del; and, because he was so easily allowing himself to be exploited, they didn't like Neal either. For all the film's brilliant comedy, the audience didn't want to watch it because they didn't *like* the lead characters.

All that changed when Hughes and Hirsch re-inserted a scene that had been filmed but left out of the film because it seemed such an inconsequential exchange. In the re-inserted scene Del offers to pay back the cost of the train ticket.

> *Del:* Just give me your address. I'll send it to you.
> *Neal [Never wanting to hear from Del again]:* No, that's okay.

At first glance, these five seconds or thirteen words don't seem that important. But although they are not vital to the plot, they are vital to the success of the film. Replacing those two lines flipped the audience's perception of the two characters. They now felt okay about Del – who is clearly *not* a freeloader – and therefore also about Neal's decision to help him.

Why we need to save a cat ... or a dog ... or an ageing Mob boss

Hirsch says he initially saw the scene as "a seemingly unimportant nuance", but this is not an unimportant nuance. Making sure that the hero is *likeable* is one of the most important features of a good story. Why would anyone want to spend two hours following the adventures of someone they don't like?

The screenwriter Blake Snyder highlighted the importance of moments like this in his book *Save the Cat!* – its quirky title coming from scenes exactly like the one that was reinserted into *Planes, Trains and Automobiles*.[5] Snyder's argument is that it doesn't really matter what the hero of the film does, even if he's a murderer or an assassin, as long as the writer inserts one scene in which the character proves himself to be essentially likeable. For example, the hero might be a ruthless gangland boss, but as long as he takes a moment to rescue a kitten from a tree on his way to a brutal killing, this simple moment signals to the audience that they're allowed to like this person and identify with them.

It sounds almost too simple, and even a bit soppy. Snyder admitted that some of his peers find it "cloying and dull". However, once you start to examine the most successful stories, you quickly realise that it is central to good popular storytelling.

Snyder gives the example of Disney's *Aladdin*. In the original story, Aladdin is a spoilt, lazy thief – not immediately someone an audience will like or want to identify with. So the screenwriters inserted an early scene where Aladdin steals food for himself but ends up giving it to two starving children. Now we like him.

When we look at great films in this light, we can quickly identify the Save the Cat moments. Indeed, sometimes they are far longer than mere moments. If *The Wizard of Oz* had started with the colour scenes in Oz itself, audiences might have struggled to identify with this odd cast of characters. But the whole of the first 20 minutes of the film is about Dorothy saving her dog Toto. It establishes Dorothy as a good, kind, likeable person whose adventures we therefore wish to follow.

Many critics believe that the critical scene in *The Godfather* is when Michael Corleone emerges from the restaurant toilet to shoot two men, but if that was the critical scene, all we would have would be a story about a military hero turning into a gangster. Why would we sympathise or identify with that?

The really important scene – the Save the Cat moment – happens earlier when Michael visits the hospital and finds his father, the Godfather, abandoned by his guards and entirely vulnerable to assassination by his gangland rivals. Michael is unarmed and not part of the Mafia world. But with quick thinking and a cool nerve he saves his father. And before he does so, he leans across the Godfather's hospital bed – and, in a moving reversal of the parent and child roles, he whispers:

> Just lie here, Pop. I'll take care of you now. I'm with you now. I'm with you ...

And now, instead of a film about a hero being dragged into a world of crime, we have a film about a brave and loving young man with everything ahead of him sacrificing his future to look after his father.

Snyder summed up the importance of Save the Cat like this:

> Though you don't have to have a scene in every movie where the hero literally saves a cat, helps an old lady across the street, or gets splashed by water at the street corner to make us love him, you must take the audience by the hand every time out and get them in sync with your main character and your story. ... If you don't, ... if you assume we'll like your main character – just cuz – you're not doing your job.

When you take the lessons you've learned from storytelling and apply them to your business communications you won't need to save a cat as such, but you will need to remember that fundamental idea: "You must take the audience by the hand every time out and get them in sync with your story." People won't listen to your stories "just cuz"; you have to make them want to.

So now, as well as the rules that define the structure of the story, we have three additional rules.

- A story usually involves change and learning.
- A story must be about our audience, not about us.
- We must actively *do something* to make our audience want to listen to our story – otherwise they won't.

In the next chapter we'll examine how all these elements of storytelling can be applied to your business communications. And learn the workplace equivalent of saving a cat.

3

Storytelling at work

**Identifying the best way to apply storytelling to our
business communications; the storytelling techniques that
won't work at work; the things about writing you learned
at school that you need to unlearn right now; and why
"What do we want to say?" is never the right place to start**

It's the night of the 2003 Emmys – the most prestigious TV
awards ceremony – and Phil Rosenthal is worried. Rosenthal,
the co-creator of the sitcom *Everybody Loves Raymond*, knows
what's going to happen because the same thing has happened
in 1999, 2000, 2001 and 2002.

In each of those years, *Everybody Loves Raymond* has been
nominated for Outstanding Comedy Series, and in each of those
years Rosenthal has dealt with the nervous tension that builds
in the months between the nominations and the ceremony
itself by obsessing over what he will say if the programme
wins. After all, he's supposed to be a funny guy, right? So his
acceptance speech had better be good.

And every year Rosenthal has sat there on the night, the
tension building further within him, agonising over the fear
that he might forget his funny speech, until finally ... the
announcement. And the horrible deflating reality that some
other programme has won.

But 2003 is destined to be different. This time, the winner is announced – and it's *Raymond*! Okay, all the worrying is finally going to pay off. Rosenthal is going to knock this industry crowd dead with his brilliant speech. After all those years of hurt, now is his time to shine.

He mounts the stage; he reaches the microphone. He looks out at the audience, and he sees a 20-foot screen that is flashing three simple words: "Wrap it up!"

You may well be aware that, at awards presentations like the Oscars and the Emmys, there is "wrap it up" music which begins to play quietly if a thank-you speech goes on too long. It then rises rapidly and dramatically in volume if the speaker doesn't take the hint. You probably didn't know that at the Emmys there is also a flashing sign that reads "Wrap it up", which is switched on pretty much as the winner takes the stage. Just as each talented individual arrives to acknowledge this extraordinary highpoint in their career, they are told to keep it short, shut up and sit down.

When you have lovingly crafted a fabulous PowerPoint presentation or other business communication, spending days or perhaps even weeks getting it just right, you can find yourself imagining that your audience is really looking forward to everything you have to say. Reluctantly, however, I have to burst your bubble. One of the key questions in everybody's mind as you begin is: "When is this going to end?"

Offices do not routinely use "wrap it up" music, and I have only once in my career been faced with a "wrap it up" sign (at a global advertising industry conference; it didn't literally say "wrap it up" but the bright red LED clock counting down to zero and bedecked with flashing lights on the podium and directed straight into the speaker's eyes made the meaning clear enough). However, although no one is yelling "wrap it up" in your ear, I urge you to think how many times in your career, when you were in the audience, you found yourself wishing a presentation would go on longer? Not many, right?

This sobering thought should shape all your storytelling at work.

Now you have a clearer idea of what a story is, how a story is constructed and the elements that need to be included, it's time to think about exactly how to use this knowledge at work. This chapter distinguishes clearly between those story elements that can be effectively applied to work communications and those techniques that aren't appropriate.

Inspired by Rosenthal's experience, let's begin with endings.

What works #1:
A beginning, a middle and (crucially) an end

All your work should have a clear beginning, middle and end. Of these three sections, having absolute clarity about your end point is the most vital.

In a brilliant episode of the sitcom *Everybody Loves Raymond* – one that Rosenthal himself wrote – the titular character gives his difficult parents Marie and Frank an annual subscription to the Fruit of the Month Club as a birthday gift. This popular gifting solution proves distinctly less than popular with his mother.

When the first consignment arrives, Marie is already confused. "There's so many of them. There's over a dozen pears! What am I supposed to do with all those pears?"

When she discovers that a new, different fruit will arrive every month, she is horrified. "Every month!" Marie rushes out of the room in terror. "I can't talk! There's too much fruit in the home."

Although this scene draws its humour from comic

exaggeration, Rosenthal based it on an actual event in his life, and there is a human truth that lurks beneath Marie's panic. It is therefore a good idea to keep Marie's reaction in mind when you are writing something. Does what you're writing just go on and on and on? If so, your audience may react (a little bit) like Marie, wondering "When is it going to end?"

This question operates on two levels. First, how long is this communication? Everyone you talk to (or ask to read a document) is busy. Very busy. And they have also experienced many overlong and extremely dull communications before. They come to your presentation not with a skip in their step and a feeling of excitement, but with reluctance, trepidation, maybe even dread. Not because you're not interesting and entertaining (remember Bette Midler, Julia Roberts and Cuba Gooding Jr are just a few of the stars who have received the "wrap it up" music, and you couldn't argue that they're not entertaining) but because they simply have so much else to do.

Then there is the second meaning of "When is this going to end?" Perhaps your presentation will have an "ask" in it – something you want them to do, or some new process that you are introducing. How long and complicated is *that*? When will *that* end?

It's vital when communicating that your audience has a clear idea both of when your communication is going to end and also of when any actions that you are asking them to get involved in are going to end.

A communication that wanders from subject to subject with no clear signals to the audience of how much more there is going to be immediately instils negative emotions in your audience. A communication that asks people to get behind or get involved in a project or process or system or solution that seems equally never-ending will also invoke a negative response. Your audience shuts down, your message is lost. They're not interested.

The value of storytelling here is that it reminds you to create a beginning and a middle and a very clear end point. As you begin your communication, you must make it clear what and where the end is. And the subject of your communication must have a clear end point too.

If you are proposing a change to working practices that will have benefits for many years to come, that's great; but nobody who's going to listen to or read your communication is judged on "many years to come". Their performance is judged right now. They need to see a clear end point – a clear result – within a timeframe that makes sense to them given their career trajectory. You not only have to offer them value – you have to offer them value *right now* that will help them in their next evaluation and help them get their next promotion (or avoid being in the next wave of redundancies).

If they have to deliver results this year, your communication must offer value to them this year. If they have to deliver results this quarter, your communication must offer value to them this quarter.

What works #2:
Unity of action

Focusing your communications on one clear message will make everything you say and write significantly more impactful and memorable.

The speaker who begins "I've got several points I want to cover this afternoon" or the document that lands on the desk with a thud or that strains the limits of your email elicits a heavy sigh in the audience or recipient.

Sometimes, of course, we just do have a lot of things we have to cover. Or at least we think we do. But this idea usually derives from the belief that communication is about saying something rather than about saying something that will actually be heard and understood.

People will not remember multiple messages, so there is little point in communicating them. If you absolutely *have* to cover several points in a piece of communication, be very clear what your most important point is and make that first and last and clearest. Everything else should be subsidiary to it. Stories can have sub-plots; but the audience should always be clear about which is the main plot.

"What do we want to say?" is always the wrong place to start

This raises a much broader point about the creation of any piece of communication. The question "What do I want to say?" or "What do we want to say?" is always the wrong place to start when writing something. Unfortunately, it's where many people choose to start. Why? Mainly because it's the easiest place to start; but it will not lead to an effective piece of communication.

Instead, the question we want to start with is some variant on "What do we want?":

What do we want to happen after this piece of communication?

What do we want the audience to do after they have listened to us?

What do we want our audience to think after they have read this document?

What do we want our audience to feel as they listen to us?

There are certain other related questions that we also need to answer:

Who are the audience?

What matters to them?

How can we offer them value?

Where are they now in relation to the subject we're discussing? (Enthusiastic? Indifferent? Actively hostile?)

What can we offer them that will move them from where they are to where we want them to be?

Note that these questions are very similar to the questions you would ask yourself in compiling any basic business strategy or indeed tactical plan:

Where are we now?

Where do we want to be?

How are we going to get there?

But instead of moving the business in a certain direction, we are talking about moving the audience in a certain direction.

If "What do I want to say?" is a bad place to start, "What do *we* want to say?" is worse. When a group sit down to write something and begin with the question "Okay, what do we want to say?", everybody throws in something, either because they have a particular bugbear they want to make sure gets in or because they need to be seen to be contributing. This inevitably leads to an unfocused presentation or document. Groups tasked with creating a piece of communication should steer away from "What do we want to say?" and towards "What are we trying to achieve?"

What works #3:
The hero's journey

It's vital in any communication to identify a clear quest and an identifiable destination.

This isn't a destination for you, but where the audience will get to if they do whatever it is you're asking them to do, believe whatever it is you're asking them to believe, or soak up the knowledge that you're giving them.

In other words, there must be a clear benefit or value for the audience listening to or reading what you have to say.

Nobody cares about your ideas (sorry)

This provocative subheading refers to a fundamental misunderstanding of what communication at work is (or what communication at work should do) which many people carry with them: that writing documents or presentations is about communicating ideas.

The reason that so many people have this fundamental misunderstanding (you may, right now, be thinking that surely it *is* about communicating ideas) is because they were taught it at school or at college.

Except in rare circumstances, people at work aren't very interested in what you have to say. They want to know what's in it for them.

I have found, when training and coaching storytelling, that, paradoxically, it can sometimes be easier to work with people who say they can't write or who believe that they aren't good at writing than to work with people who believe that they are already good writers. This is because the latter group are often good at writing in a particular way – the way that is taught at school and college – and this does not equate to good business writing.

When you start writing in business, you have to let go of almost everything you knew about writing before.

Why is this? Because when you are at school, your writing is judged against very specific criteria and these are not the criteria against which your writing will be judged or valued in a business setting.

If you write an essay at school or college, your essay will be judged based on your ability to transmit ideas to the reader.

In a business setting, good writing doesn't transmit ideas, it transmits value. Larry McEnerney, former head of the University of Chicago writing programme, puts it like this:

> Yes, your writing needs to be clear, organised, persuasive. But more than anything else, your writing needs to be valuable. Because if it's not, nothing else matters, it makes zero difference.
>
> If it's clear and useless, it's useless. If it's organised and useless, it's useless. If it's persuasive and useless, it's useless.
>
> Value is determined by the community – this is why writing is about readers, and not about content. Value lies in readers, not in the writing.

Your writing, like a story, must have a quest – and the subject of that quest is something useful or valuable or beneficial to the audience. You must make clear to the audience from the beginning what that benefit is. *That* is why they will pay attention: not because you have great ideas, not because you express them beautifully, but because what you are going to say to them will be useful. You are, in Joseph Campbell's words, offering them a boon or a gift.

One of the ironies of business communication in large organisations is that the task of the most important presentations and documents is often handed to the strategic thinkers. These are the people who throughout their time at school and college have earned good grades and have been told that they are very good at writing. They trade in the currency of ideas. And their writing is often all about the communication of those ideas. It therefore may not be very effective business communication. It will be of interest to other strategic thinkers in the same industry, perhaps, but that is almost certainly not the audience that they are trying to reach.

It's not a terrible idea to give writing tasks to strategic thinkers: they tend to be adept with words. But it is usually a good idea to take the writing task away from them before the final draft, and hand it to someone whose task is to make sure that their elegant writing is also useful to the audience.

What works #4:
The problem/solution structure

Your statement of value to the audience – the unveiling of the destination for your quest – gives a natural beginning and end to your communication: the delivery of value is the end, and the upfront statement of what you will deliver is the beginning. How then do we get from the beginning to the end? What is our middle? Fortunately, the problem/solution structure which forms the basis of good stories is perfectly suited and easily adapted to the business environment. It will guide and give shape to our middle.

Work, as you will have realised by now, is a series of problems all of which need solutions, so the easiest part of any business writing is to ask: what are the problems? The slightly less easy part is: what are we going to do about them? The solutions.

If your communication is going to be a presentation and if you're going to deliver it in person, then Grebanier's Proposition comes into play. You can bring the problem/solution structure vividly to life, and maintain and direct the attention of the audience where you want it, using a series of questions and answers. Each slide is linked to the next by verbally summarising the conclusion of the former and framing the (hopefully obvious) next question, which should now be in your audience's minds and which your next slide will answer.

Now that we have all the data, what does it tell us?

As we've seen, we're losing customers to our competitors. What are the main reasons that they are dissatisfied with our service?

So far, our plan to roll out the new ways of working globally has stalled. Which countries are proving the most obstinate?

Okay, so we've identified the most reluctant countries. What reasons are they giving for failing to adopt the new ways of working?

We're meeting resistance because we're told our new processes are not a cultural fit in this territory. Have we been culturally insensitive and how can we remedy this?

Many business presentations lend themselves perfectly to this kind of structure. Using questions as a navigation device gives storytelling shape to your presentation. It also offers a quick catch-up to anyone whose focus has drifted for a moment. As a bonus it makes presenting much easier for those who find the task daunting (because each slide leads naturally, inevitably, from the previous one, there is far less danger of suddenly getting "lost"). And finally, it helps us to take the reader out of their inner monologue, which as you'll see in the next chapter, is something you need to do.

What works #5:
The story spine

It is also possible to populate the middle of your communication using Pixar's method (or, as it should perhaps be known, Kenn Adams's story spine), rather than a series of questions, to give storytelling shape and structure to your content.

This approach is particularly helpful if you are writing by committee because, thanks to the huge popularity of Pixar films, the enduring global appeal of classic Disney films and the cultural ubiquity of the fairy stories on which many of them are based, the "Once upon a time ..." structure is quicky grasped by almost everyone.

Of course you will (almost certainly) choose not actually to say "Once upon a time .../ every day .../ because of that .../ and ever since then ..." out loud when you tell your story. This structure is the scaffolding you use to build the story and, as with scaffolding on a building, you remove it once the story is finished.

What works #6
Under pressure, we learn

Good business communications will often involve change: you're asking somebody to do something new or different, or to stop doing something.

There are exceptions, but even in a situation where your brief has been simply to "present all the data" or "provide a quick summary of progress so far" (if your audience has expressly asked for exposition, facts and data), if you can find insight in the data that could suggest meaningful change or a negative change that threatens the business, then you have a story. And you have a much more interested audience.

Similarly, if your story can help the audience to understand or learn something that they didn't understand or know before, again you have the makings of a story, because learning is integral to good stories.

The storytelling element that "under pressure, we learn" is something that can definitely transfer to our business storytelling. However, it has to be handled extremely carefully because telling somebody something they don't know can easily become patronising or condescending. It's especially tricky if you are speaking to an audience who are more senior than you are. At times like this, it's a good idea to take the advice of Baltasar Gracián.

Born in Spain in 1601, Gracián was a Jesuit priest and a famous preacher. Although his unorthodox methods often caused him to be reprimanded by his superiors (he once read a letter from the pulpit which he said had been sent from Hell), he was a wily political operator who always knew how to stay just the right side of the line.

His writings have gained the admiration of philosophers such as Schopenhauer and Nietzsche. *The Art of Worldly Wisdom* is perhaps his most famous work (and, in this context, it's worth noting that a more literal translation of the Spanish title would be *The Art of Discretion*).

It contains 300 maxims to help the reader get ahead in life, and many of them still resonate today. Gracián is cited over 25 times in #1 best-selling self-help book *The 48 Laws of Power* by Robert Greene; his wisdom includes lines such as "Never compete with a man who has nothing to lose" and "A wise man gets more use from his enemies than a fool from his friends." But the advice that's most relevant to us here is:

> Avoid outshining the master. All superiority is odious, but the superiority of a subject over his prince is not only stupid, it is fatal. This is a lesson that the stars in the sky teach us – they may be related to the sun, and just as brilliant, but they never appear in her company.

When you know something that your audience doesn't know – even if they have brought you into the meeting especially for your knowledge and expertise – it is usually a good idea to suggest that you are simply recounting something they already know, or at least something they would have realised instantly if they had access to the same data as you. As Gracián put it:

> When you counsel someone, you should appear to be reminding him of something he had forgotten, not of the light he was unable to see.

For "someone", substitute "client", "customer", "line manager", "the board" or "CEO" as appropriate. The principle remains the same. Whenever you find that you have the impulse to be the smartest person in the room, take a deep breath, let the impulse pass, and allow everyone else to feel smart instead.

Storytelling drives change

Fortunately, the storytelling structure closely aligns with what we know about behaviour change models.

We know, for example, that to drive behaviour change, it's important to offer a clear vision of a positive future that lies beyond the behaviour change. If all you do is explain what's wrong with the current situation, people will intellectually get the need for change but be reluctant to do it. Seeing a brighter future ahead is more motivating, and a clear vision of a positive future is at the heart of storytelling.

Similarly, behaviour change models tend to emphasise the importance of offering clear step-by-step guides to progress towards the desired behaviour change (people are more likely to adopt a healthier diet if they are given simple, affordable recipes using healthy foods than if they are merely told what's wrong with their present eating patterns). This approach can be closely mirrored by adopting the problem/solution structure of stories.

What works #7
Telling their story, not your story

In business communications the most important relationship has to be the one you have with your audience, not the one you have with your content.

As already established, your communications must have value or benefit to your audience, and who determines whether this is so? Obviously, your audience does. Not you.

John Steinbeck's idea that "If a story is not about the hearer, he will not listen" is entirely applicable to the workplace.

If your audience cannot see that you're talking about them and offering value to them, they will disengage very quickly indeed. That's why we must never be the hero of our own story, however counterintuitive that may seem.

And it does seem counterintuitive. How about when someone has asked to see your company's "creds", or when a prospect says, "Tell me about your product", or when someone very high up in the firm asks you to explain what you and your team does? Surely, then, you have to make the story about you, your team or your product?

No, because "Tell me about your company" means "Tell

me what your company can do for me and my company." "Tell me about your product" means "Tell me how your product will help me and my company." And "Tell me about you/your team" means "Explain to me again how you and your team are adding value to me/making my life easier/making money for the company." The real question that is being asked is always some variant on "How do you/could you add value to me?"

Okay, but how about when we have actually done something heroic? What about when we've gone that extra mile to deliver a report? What about when we've undercut all our competitor's pricing in a special one-time deal for this client? What about when our algorithm really does outshine the competition? Can't we be the hero then?

Not really. The fact is that even real-life, genuine, gold-plated heroes shouldn't be the heroes of their own story. A vivid example of this truth was shown when John Kerry ran against the incumbent George W. Bush for the US presidency in 2004.

John Kerry is a hero.

He received two Purple Hearts, a Silver Star and a Bronze Star for his heroism during the Vietnam War (whereas Bush was seen as having used his father's political influence to avoid conscription into the army). So perhaps it's not surprising that Kerry chose to use his heroic military career prominently in his speeches. Clearly it was an area where he could prove his demonstrable superiority to his opponent. That's what winning an election is about, right?

No, it isn't. And neither is selling a product about proving your superiority to your competitor. That's the "building a logical argument" fallacy that we dismissed in Chapter 1. You might win the intellectual argument, but you won't win hearts. You will push your audience away.

Basically, Kerry talked about himself whereas Bush talked

about what Americans have achieved and what Americans could achieve. Kerry's speeches tended to be about his story; Bush's speech tended to be about "their story".

If you are the hero of your own story, you leave little room for anyone else. Even if there is room for them, you've already relegated them to being a sidekick.

When you tell stories in business, *you* are the sidekick. You are there to help your audience, who must always be the hero (or heroes).

What works #8: Storytelling language

Unless you're reading this book on your first day in your first job, someone will already have told you to avoid using jargon in your communications. Let's take it further than that. Let's make it absolutely clear that – except when drawing up a contract or other legal document – there is no excuse for doing anything other than writing down your communication exactly as you would say it.

Storytelling language is the language that we speak to each other in ordinary conversations.

If you stick to normal, everyday language, you are already communicating storytelling to your audience. The minute you slip into jargon, and business-y phrases, you are leaving the language of storytelling and entering the language of bullet points and logical arguments.

The way to ensure that you adhere to this rule is to practise reading everything you write out loud. Not in your head, *literally* out loud. If it doesn't come naturally off your tongue, it isn't right.

*

There is clearly much that we can apply directly from the storytelling we find in novels and films to business storytelling. But what are the elements of storytelling that won't translate readily into the work environment?

*

What *doesn't* work #1:
Tease and reveal

A masterful storyteller working in the arts will hold back key information from the audience to build suspense or induce mystery. In the workplace, this isn't exciting. It's annoying.

In a document or presentation, teasing the audience, or (as it's sometimes known) creating "knowledge gaps", is irritating in the extreme.

A successful thriller writer will leave a cliff-hanger at the end of Chapter 1, spend Chapter 2 dealing with a sub-plot and only come back to resolve the cliff-hanger in Chapter 3. They will, meanwhile, have left another cliff-hanger at the end of Chapter 2, which won't be dealt with until Chapter 4. In this way, they maintain the interest of the reader throughout the book.

It's not an easy skill to master, and there's no reason why you should have mastered it. So make things easier for yourself. Do not try to tease and reveal. Do not try to create mystery and suspense.

If you get it wrong, you're simply going to alienate your audience.

Intriguingly, the (admittedly limited) research into this area suggests that we like to know the ending of stories. This seems odd – after all, when someone gives the ending away it's called a "spoiler" not an "enhancer" – but it's worth noting.

Research has been conducted using stories from authors including the queen of the whodunnit Agatha Christie.[1] Some people were given the stories to read with an introductory text that explained the ending; others were given the stories to read with no extra information. Surprisingly, it turned out that participants preferred the "spoiled" versions over the "unspoiled" ones.

One of the researchers, psychologist Jonathan Leavitt, made this suggestion:

> Once you know how [a story] turns out, it's cognitively easier – you're more comfortable processing the information – and can focus on a deeper understanding.

Writing about this "spoiler paradox", the psychologist Adoree Durayappah said: "So this means that a spoiler is not really a spoiler at all. It takes a complex story and simplifies it, allowing you to process it easier."[2]

If you have a complicated message to communicate, it is clearly worth considering that if you explain the end point of your communication first, you make it easier for your audience to follow the complexities of your argument.

What *doesn't* work #2: Rambling anecdotes

One of the unfortunate consequences of storytelling becoming such a buzzword in business is that many people suffer from the mistaken assumption that storytelling simply means kicking off every presentation with a personal anecdote.

This misapprehension is responsible for some of the most cringe-inducing presentations and dismal TED talks out there. The ones that begin something like: "I was 12 years old and helping my dad out in the family hardware store. To begin with my job was just sweeping the floor and stacking the shelves, but I swept that floor with pride!"

The speaker has heard that storytelling is a good thing, and has probably also read somewhere that opening up and sharing is a good thing too. Yes, it is good to share. Sometimes. If you're putting together a new project team, it can be beneficial to open up to each other as this will help the team bond (under the auspices of a well-trained facilitator, anyway; poorly planned do-it-yourself sessions where people are encouraged to allow themselves to be vulnerable are as likely to wreck as to bond a team). Sharing a personal story can sometimes be part of this bonding process, but sharing a personal story is not the best way to open most business communications.

If you think it will be helpful to illustrate the point you're making with an anecdote, make it an anecdote that follows the story structure outlined in Chapter 2, and one in which the audience (or someone to whom the audience can immediately relate) is the hero.

The only time that something that happened to *you* should be used to illustrate a point you're making is if you're pretty certain that it (or something very like it) has happened to many of your audience as well. I am not suggesting that your experience isn't important; of course it is. But it isn't necessarily the best vehicle to use when communicating with others, and will often obscure rather than clarify your message.

What *doesn't* work #3
Doing all the talking

It seems pretty much axiomatic that storytelling must be a one-way communication. However, even if you are literally doing all the talking, you must make every effort to create the sense that what is happening is a conversation.

Research shows that one of the factors that most strongly determine whether someone thinks a meeting has gone well is how much they talked. They don't need to dominate the meeting, they don't need to get their own way all the time, but they do need to feel heard. So if your presentations consist of you talking and everybody else listening, clearly you are creating potential problems for yourself. We might even say that the conventional format of "a presentation" as it is generally understood in many companies seems to contain a fatal flaw: the audience will not think they've talked a lot for the very good reason that they haven't, and therefore they will be less likely to think the meeting has gone well.

You must find a way to turn your presentations – your stories – into something more akin to a dialogue.

The most obvious way to do this – and the way that is most routinely employed – is to leave room for the audience to ask questions. This seems simple enough, but people who write their presentations from a basis of "What do I want to say?" always tend to want to cram as much content in as possible. They often find that they overrun, and the time notionally left aside for "questions at the end" gets squeezed. They feel that their job is done – they have, after all "landed all their points" – so don't realise that little real communication has taken place and that their audience is fundamentally feeling that this has not been a good meeting.

Hopefully, if you have read this far, you realise that "landing points" is about as far from storytelling as you can get and is not a good model for true communication. If you have mentally reduced your audience to a strip of tarmac that will lie there and have points landed on it, you are reducing your ability to build a relationship with them, are unlikely to engage or enthuse them, and probably won't win them over to your point of view (or indeed sell them anything).

The first way we can improve on this is by not constraining our audience's participation to a brief moment at the end of the meeting. "We'll leave questions till the end, if that's okay" is a sentence that should be avoided wherever possible. It should be made clear that questions are welcome at any stage.

When I teach this, I naturally meet resistance from some people who fear that they will be "derailed" by questions and that they will therefore not "land" all their points. Deftly ignoring the confused transport metaphors, I explain that this is a small price to pay for some genuine human interaction; that they are not being "derailed" but being given a chance to communicate more deeply.

Even when told they can speak freely, people can still be reluctant to "interrupt" someone. So regular reminders and prompts that you welcome questions are necessary.

If you know your audience, you can invite questions personally. "Amanda, I know this is an area that interests you. Do you have any comments at this point?"

Arguably, the best way to create a *sense* of conversation is by anticipating your audience's inner voice and articulating it for them. You ask the questions on their behalf.

As you're showing them slide two, what do you expect them to be thinking? That should be the subject of slide three. This takes us back into the area of Grebanier's Proposition: being aware of the question that is probably being generated by what we're saying; asking that question (being, in effect, the voice of our audience); and then answering it.

If you can employ this question/answer format and bring your audience's inner dialogue to life for them, even though they have not actually spoken, they will feel heard.

Researchers who have looked into story-generation software have focused on exactly this: the point of interaction between the story and the reader. What does each sentence of the story *do* to the reader; what questions does it raise in their mind; and how can that inform the next sentence?

This is what storytelling is, right at the sharp end, where the story meets the audience. Paul Bailey from the artificial intelligence department at the University of Edinburgh, wrote a fascinating paper titled "Searching for storiness", which explores the audience's contribution to the story.[3] In the paper he includes this insight from Dona Cooper:

> The energy to process a story is the result of *questions* forming in the audience's negative space in reaction to story information. The audience members ask themselves questions in order to get themselves oriented, work their way through a myriad of information, and figure out what's important and what's not.
>
> Additionally, the audience will not only have questions, but their minds will attempt to provide possible answers as well.[4]

In an article published in the *Proceedings of the National Academy of Sciences*, researchers Lauren Silbert and co-workers discussed their study which employed functional magnetic resonance imaging (fMRI) brain scans to record brain activity from both speakers and listeners during verbal communication.[5]

They found that the speaker's activity is spatially and temporarily coupled with the listener's activity, but that this coupling disappears when participants fail to communicate effectively. Intriguingly, although the listener's brain activity usually mirrors the speaker's brain activity with a very slight delay, there are also times when the listener's brain *anticipates* rather than follows the speaker's brain activity. The greater the anticipatory coupling, the greater the understanding.

This appears to show that when the listener is just one step ahead of the speaker, they understand communication in more depth and detail. It's an unexpected model for communication – and, once again, goes against any desire we might have to be the dominant force or smartest person in the room when we're presenting. Rather than revealing our exceptional wisdom, fascinating data and brilliant ideas to a passive, receptive audience, we will communicate much better if we are merely leading them towards a conclusion that they are making just ahead of us.

There are a handful of storytelling techniques that should be avoided at work, but most of the ideas outlined in the previous chapter transfer well. Every major work presentation or document should have a beginning, a middle and an end. It should have unity of action – it should be about one thing. It can be structured using the hero's journey or the story spine, but either way it should incorporate the ups and downs of the problem/solution story structure.

And, speaking of problems and solutions, there are a few problems that you will probably encounter when you try to bring storytelling to life at work. The next chapter takes you through them and outlines how they can be overcome.

4

What gets in the way of good storytelling?

Avoiding the major pitfalls to great storytelling; conquering our nemesis (it's PowerPoint) via storytelling headlines; and understanding the potential dangers of "our tiny skull-sized kingdoms"

If Whitfield Diffie hadn't had more important things to do, PowerPoint could have turned out to be a brilliant storytelling tool. But he did. And so it didn't.

Diffie is a pioneer of modern cryptography, and, with colleague Martin Hellman, won the 2015 Turing Award, the most prestigious award in the field of computer science. Their work underpins the security protocols of the internet.

Back in 1981, while working at Bell-Northern Research, Diffie was preparing to give a presentation, which, in those days, was on 35 mm slides. He knew that a colleague had created a simple program that allowed you to draw a black frame on a piece of paper. Playing with this, Diffie adapted the program so that it would create a series of rectangular frames, with space for a small amount of text inside and further block of adjacent text. He had, essentially, created a program to build a template for a storyboard, and laid the first inspiration for PowerPoint.

But Diffie had no interest in taking his idea further, nor (he later admitted) did he see the potential in it. If he had done, then perhaps PowerPoint could have developed into software perfectly designed for storytelling.

Although Diffie didn't see any future in his idea, Bell-Northern's head of computer science research Robert Gaskins was inspired by it. Three years later, after he had moved to Silicon Valley software firm Forethought, Gaskins hired a software developer, Dennis Austin, and began developing a product they originally called Presenter, but which the world would later know as PowerPoint.

But here's the crucial point. Diffie's storyboard – essentially akin to the "slide sorter" view of PowerPoint – is a perfect visual entry point for storytelling. But how many people begin creating a PowerPoint presentation in "slide-sorter" view? Not many. The product that Gaskins developed was something quite different.

For many years, I mistakenly assumed that PowerPoint was *supposed* to be a storytelling tool; it had just been designed very badly. It turns out this is not the case. Gaskins specifically designed PowerPoint to be a *summarising* tool. His vision was that people would present their case verbally, backed up by lengthy, detail-rich documents. They would then quickly *summarise* the key points using PowerPoint. The original business pitch for PowerPoint itself was a 53-page document, supplemented by a relatively brief 12-slide summary.

PowerPoint's bullet-pointed lists are ideally suited to that task. But not to the task for which most people actually use it.

Why is it so hard to tell stories?

If storytelling language is basically the language that we use every day, and therefore much of our normal conversation with friends and family consists of telling each other stories, why is it so hard to tell stories at work? Why does there need to be a book on the subject? Why do we need to follow a process?

Partly the answer is that, while we do indeed use storytelling structure in our everyday conversations with those close to us, we do so in an abbreviated form based on a shared body of knowledge and understanding built up over years in each relationship. We don't, for example, have to "save the cat" in each story to align with our audience – we work on the basis that our friends will automatically like and sympathise with us because they are our friends.

This won't translate to our workplace. It might do in a few informal situations with friendly colleagues, of course, but not in the big documents and presentations that really matter.

Another reason is that one of the most powerful and ubiquitous business communications tools seems to have been designed expressly to stop us from telling stories, and instead lead us into an anti-storytelling world of bullet-pointed lists. In fact, it *was* designed to do just that.

The fact that the phrase "death by PowerPoint" has entered the business lexicon is a measure of how terrible presentations using PowerPoint can be. It seems silly to blame the software though. Surely the fault lies with the people who use it. Isn't it a case of: PowerPoint doesn't bore people; *people* bore people?

But despite being mindful of the whole bad workman/tools dynamic, the truth is somewhere in between. I'm going to argue that much of the poor communication that gets delivered via PowerPoint truly *is* the fault of the software.

PowerPoint actually tells people to communicate badly.

How to avoid "Death by PowerPoint": storytelling headlines

The ubiquitous software – now widely and horribly used for documents as well as presentations – has come to define the way many people, and entire corporations, communicate. Why? Because as an *executional* medium it is excellent. Once you know exactly what your slide should be, PowerPoint will make it easily and quickly. It does the job intuitively and well.

Sadly, though, it does the wrong job.

Subtly and not so subtly it guides the user to communicate in a way that is almost the exact opposite of storytelling. It does the job Gaskins designed it to do nearly 40 years ago very well indeed. It's an excellent summariser. But despite the fact that, over those 40 years, people have routinely used it not to summarise but to build their entire presentation, it has never really evolved to reflect this fact. It is, effectively, the wrong tool for the job that we all use it for. It is therefore our nemesis. We must tame PowerPoint's excesses and only then will we be able to use its undoubted executional power for good.

There are many possible slide formats available, and many companies create their own templates; but in general terms, if you open a new slide in PowerPoint you are likely to be given two instructions:

Click to add title

and

Click to add text

except the second one is often actually this:

- *Click to add text*

And, in those two simple instructions PowerPoint steers you away from storytelling.

Let's deal with the text first. Even if the version that you are using doesn't automatically default to putting a bullet point at the start of every line, the odds are you grew up using slides that did. Thanks to this default, and the fact that you've seen innumerable slides created by other people, it's hard to create – and you rarely ever see – a slide presentation that doesn't over-rely on bullet-points.

Why is this bad? In Chapter 1 we saw that lists aren't memorable, and that building up a logical argument is a sub-optimal way of writing a presentation. Bullet points are, by nature, a list; they are the natural habitat of logical arguments. They kill the causal flow that breathes life into storytelling.

Bullet points are not *always* bad. Sometimes a list is useful – usually as a summary – and of course we do need to know what our logical argument is. Used sparingly, bullet points have their place. But they will almost inevitably interrupt your storytelling flow, so need to be employed with extreme care, and not (as PowerPoint seems to suggest) dropped in at every available opportunity.

Let's move on to:

Click to add title

Sounds harmless enough. So what's wrong with it?

Titles are the death of storytelling. They stop our story dead and turn it back into a business argument. They make it harder for you to present your slides and harder for your audience to understand them.

They are also, quite simply, a waste of space and time.

To use PowerPoint (or any other slide software) successfully, you need to replace titles with what I term "storytelling headlines". These are, exactly as the name suggests, headlines that tell your story.

So what is the difference between a title and a storytelling headline? To explain it, let me use a silly example. It has to be a silly example because I want to emphasise how silly – and utterly pointless – conventional slide titles are.

Imagine I'm working as part of a team and we're about to give a presentation. It's a long deck, but I personally have to deliver only one slide. I've done my homework, and I know that what my audience needs to know is exactly where the cat was five minutes ago. (I warned you it was silly.) The key message of my slide, then, is that famous kindergarten sentence:

The cat sat on the mat

This is the key point that I need to communicate; my audience needs to know where the cat was and I can tell them. And because that is my key message and because that is exactly how I would say it out loud, that is also my storytelling headline. My storytelling headline for my one and only slide should read:

The cat sat on the mat

Simple. So how could this possibly go wrong? Well, what normally happens is something like this. I open PowerPoint and I see a box that says "Click to add title". (Or even if I don't, I've become so accustomed to the idea that I know I'm supposed to put a title here.) And I think to myself ... oh right ... um ... what title should I give this slide?

I know what a title is. I've seen thousands of them over the years. They say things like "About us" or "Challenges and goals" or "Our solution" or "Potential markets" or "Headwinds and tailwinds" or "Benefits". They're short and snappy, and they tell you what the slide is going to be about.

So then I might say, well ... what is this slide about? And I might decide that it's about 'where the cat was', but I'm trying to impress an audience here so I want some slightly more educated way of saying that, and I end up with the title:

Pet location

Then I remember that this presentation is aiming to sell our company to a new customer. So I think that perhaps it should be a bit more boastful. So I change it to:

Our unique insight

Then I think, hey, we're a research company and we want to show that this information is based on data. Maybe I should get the word "Research" in there somewhere. So I have another go:

Research findings: domestic animal placement

Then I get an email from the team leader stressing that all through this presentation we need to try to differentiate against our competitors through our bespoke tech. So I decide to hero the tools! And I come up with:

Benefits of our Cat Locator Plus™ algorithm

This is a silly example. But I'm prepared to bet that you have seen equivalent titles on PowerPoint slides again and again. They all derive from perfectly good ideas: you want to sound professional; you want to differentiate from the competition; you have got some good tools and systems.

And yet these titles won't help. They are all, quite literally, a waste of space. Titles perform the role of telling the audience what the slide is going to be about – and this role is not only unnecessary, but it is also harmful to communication.

It's unnecessary because the audience does not need, each

time you put up a slide, to read a sentence that tells them in very rough terms what the rest of the slide is going to be about. Why would they? The rest of the slide is right there in front of them.

It's harmful because research suggests that when you put up a new slide in a presentation, you have about five to six seconds of attention before your audience will tend to drift off and think about other things. This is not because you're boring; it is because they are human, and the human mind likes to wander. Perhaps you're a very charismatic presenter and you can maintain attention for longer than that, but you can only really be *sure* of five to six seconds of attention.

If you've put a title at the top of your slide, you've wasted those five seconds on communicating a vague idea of the rough subject matter you're about to talk about. By the time you get to your actual point, their attention has potentially gone.

Not only does it waste your five precious seconds, it also completely disrupts the causal flow between one slide and the next, which is an important part of our sense of storytelling. "The cat sat on the mat" is a phrase that can form part of a story. "Pet locations" isn't. More to the point, neither are "About us", "Challenges and goals", "Our solution", "Potential markets", "Headwinds and tailwinds", "Benefits" or any of the other titles that people put on slides.

How do storytelling headlines differ from traditional titles?

So what is the distinction between a title and a storytelling headline? The storytelling headline conveys the key message of the slide – the piece of information that conveys the most *value* to the audience. If after reading the headline your audience tunes out, checks their emails or just daydreams about dinner, it's not a disaster. They have already taken in the most important thing you have to say to them.

A title, meanwhile, wilfully ignores the key message of the slide and instead tells the audience nothing that they need or want to know. It has no value for the audience. It is therefore a complete waste of time.

In a storytelling headline, you communicate your key message. Everything else afterwards is the context that supports that message.

Shouldn't the context come first? Shouldn't we build towards our main point? No. Because although the context is interesting to you (because you know what it is the context *to*), it is not interesting to your audience, who are wondering "Why the hell are they telling me this?" Context becomes interesting only when the value has already been established.

(This may seem counterintuitive to you, because at school or college you were encouraged to put lots of context first; but remember, the person marking your essay also knew what it was the context *to*, because they taught it to you.)

To be absolutely sure of the distinction between a traditional slide title and a storytelling headline, take a look at the following table. On the left is a series of typical titles; to the right of each is a storytelling headline that conveys in storytelling language what the main point of such a slide might be. I say "might be" because, of course, a title is too vague for us to know what point a slide is making; these are just examples to illustrate the difference.

Title	Storytelling headline
Research findings	Consumers under 30 have never heard of your brand
Benefits of our tech stack	Our data platform will let you match customer behaviour to digital behaviour more accurately
Diversity in senior management	Companies with more women on the board perform better
Test and learn	Our test-and-learn approach will help you find the best route to market
Wellbeing in the office	If you're struggling, talk to one of our trained mental health team
Costs	Last year costs grew faster than revenue
Website challenges	Your site is hard to navigate, so prospects give up
Stakeholder mapping	We aim to have regular contact with six named individuals in each of our clients

Storytelling headlines contain one key point. They tend to be a bit longer than titles, but that's okay because they are valuable to your audience. "Research findings" may be short and snappy, but the words are wasted because they say nothing of any value to the audience, and they do not continue the story. "Consumers under 30 have never heard of your brand" is nine words long, but each word has potential value to the audience.

This point is worth making because when you first start using storytelling headlines, although most people will immediately understand and appreciate the improvement, you may occasionally encounter a traditionalist who takes one quick look at your presentation, doesn't read much of it, and says "Make the headlines shorter." It's important that you push back against this feedback and explain why the slightly longer headline is justified. It's not their fault (twenty years ago someone told them to make their headlines shorter and so it's their go-to feedback comment) but it needs to be challenged because it's wrong.

How to write a storytelling headline

Writing storytelling headlines is easy. They are literally what you would say. To write them, follow the simple process shown in Figure 1 for each slide you create (or edit).

Figure 1: Writing a storytelling headline

What is the audience benefit on this slide?

If there is no audience benefit, you should probably delete the slide. If you feel you have to keep the slide, ask yourself, "What is the one thing I want the audience to know, think, do or feel after I have presented or they have read this slide?" This is your proxy audience benefit

⬇

How would I express this audience benefit if I was saying it out loud in a normal conversation with another human being?

⬇

That's your headline

⬇

Now populate the rest of the slide with the absolute minimum amount of extra information needed to justify this headline. Do not add pictures, graphics, charts or text unless they prove or explain the truth of the headline, or bring it vividly to life

⬇

Check: do you get your main point across in the first 5 seconds?

Our egos will try (really hard) to derail our story

In a brilliant commencement address delivered to the Kenyon College graduating class of 2005, novelist David Foster Wallace explained that we are all "lords of our own tiny skull-sized kingdoms" – that, inevitably, we experience our entire lives from our own blinkered and biased perspective. Because of the way we are designed, we are literally at the centre of everything we experience. We are the central character – the hero – in the story that we live out every single day of our lives. It therefore becomes one of the hardest challenges of storytelling to break out of our tiny skull-sized kingdom and to put someone else at the centre of the story.

Even when you know you should be writing from the audience's perspective, even when you have taken John Steinbeck's words to heart and understand that your story must be about the listener, the basic reality of the human condition keeps dragging you back to your own perspective. It's not enough to know intellectually that you must "tell their story, not your story". You have to continually and relentlessly fight against your natural, very human urge to slip back into telling your own story. And when you're working with a team, or with many senior stakeholders, you need processes in place to stop this happening, because all your instincts – and all the instincts of everybody in the team – will be pushing you in the wrong direction.

Just as each of us as individuals tends to put ourselves at the centre of a story, each company also exists in its own "kingdom" and will tend to revert to talking about itself. When senior stakeholders give feedback on presentations and documents, it more often than not comes in the form of "We need to say more about X" or "We need to add in something about Y", and

X and Y are almost invariably *something about ourselves*. Not about your clients, prospects, customers or whoever we ought to be making the heroes of the story.

"Are you telling their story, not your story?" is a question that should be asked about every paragraph and every slide at every stage of the writing and editing process.

Allowing our audience to retreat into their inner voice will cause us problems

Surprise, surprise: everyone that you write for or present to also lives their life in their tiny skull-sized kingdom. You cannot ever assume that you will have your audience's attention for the whole of your communication. In what psychologists term the brain's "natural resting state" the brain doesn't rest at all; modern human beings can usually focus their attention for only a few seconds before it starts to wander. It wanders forwards to lunchtime and what they're going to have, and backwards to the previous meeting and everything they should have said and done differently; it wanders forward to the weekend and their socialising plans, and bizarrely it might also wander back to a random memory from school days triggered by a word, a facial expression, a sound or a smell in the room.

It's hard work for humans to keep their brains focused on one subject for any length of time. Left to its own devices your brain would prefer to shift from subject to subject, so that's what tends to happen.

When you're the one watching a presentation or reading a document you know how easy it is to lose focus and not really take in all the content, so when you are the one authoring or presenting you have to constantly work to attract and maintain attention. You cannot allow people's minds to wander because as soon as they start to wander, they become lost inside their inner monologue, worrying about the meeting later in the day, regretting something they said in an email yesterday, trying to work out exactly what their boss meant by that comment last week. Once they're in there, listening to their inner monologue, it's very hard to get them back out again.

A storytelling structure will help to maintain attention, as will storytelling headlines. But additionally, it is vital to focus attention on the point of interaction between your story and the reader or listener: that you constantly consider what your story is doing to the reader/listener at that moment, rather than just worry about the content of what you're saying or writing. You need to think:

Where have you taken them?

What will they be thinking now?

What will be the next question in their mind?

If you can correctly identify this "next question" and answer it immediately, we increase your chances of keeping them out of their inner monologue and still paying attention to you.

Thinking that writing is easy makes it harder

Two factors that can get in the way of good storytelling are thinking that writing is easy, and thinking that writing *should* be easy.

To be brutally honest, one of the main reasons for poor business communication is that the author or authors simply haven't spent enough time on creating it. They did not devote enough time or attention to the task. Their business communication is poor because they simply haven't worked hard enough. They don't understand that good writing involves more than merely "delivering content". They assume that by saying whatever is in their head, they've done the job. This isn't the case.

Another group of people struggle for what seems like almost the opposite reason. They don't think writing is easy. In fact they find it very hard. But they make it harder for themselves by adding a layer of self-criticism. They suspect that writing *should* be easy, that other people find it easier than they do, and that they are struggling with a writing task because they're not good writers.

When these people write a first draft and are disappointed with their efforts, their conclusion is that that have failed at what should have been a fairly simple task, and therefore that they "can't write".

But the real reason that they are not finding the writing task easy is because it isn't easy.

Instead of recognising that they're facing a challenging task and that it takes time and concentration (and several drafts) they become self-critical about their performance, decide that they probably can't do any better, and end up turning in work that is below their true potential.

The novelist Thomas Mann wittily expressed the professional writer's attitude to the writing task like this:

> A writer is someone for whom writing is more difficult than it is for other people.

One of the simplest ways to improve your business communication, whether in writing or verbally, is simply to give it the dedication that it needs. When you find that you haven't finished a writing task that you feel you should have finished, don't veer into self-criticism. Instead, recalibrate your view of the task; you are not failing to complete an easy task; you are instead carefully working your way through a complex task that demands more time and thought.

But we're all busy, and there will almost certainly be a deadline involved, so it may be difficult to add time on at the end of the task. The key behaviour change needed, then, is to begin the task earlier (where possible) and ring-fence enough time in your diary not just to write what is required but to write it, sleep on it, rewrite it and ideally sleep on it again and rewrite it again.

Having a realistic expectation of how challenging a writing task can be will help you to complete that task. If you find that your writing just flows, you are either very lucky or simply deluding yourself that you are completing the task when in fact you are writing a substandard version of what is needed. Ask someone who writes for a living, how often their writing "just flows". When they've stopped laughing, ask them how many drafts they usually work through before they consider the job is done.

However, one of the philosophies of the Navy SEAL teams is: "Slow is smooth and smooth is fast." If you slow down initially and take time to put the proper structure in place for your writing, you will then find that the rest of the task becomes easier and quicker.

To help with this, the next chapter introduces the SUPERB six-step storytelling model, which you can use to structure just about any business communication, even if you're using PowerPoint to deliver it.

5

How to create great stories at work

How the SUPERB six-step storytelling model can help you create better communications at work; how each step of the model builds on the Hollywood storytelling template; and how "the sneezing baby panda of the TED ecosystem" can make sure all your stories start the right way

If Frank Sinatra hadn't injured his hand we might never have experienced one of the most frequently used storytelling tropes of the late 20th and 21st century: the rogue cop.

Sinatra was the first actor to be offered the role of Harry Callahan in a film that had the working title of *Dead Right*. But he felt that he was not up to the action scenes given a recent injury to his hand.

Dead Right was a relentless tale of a policeman who breaks the rules to end a killer's reign of terror. The script was circulating round Hollywood just as the 1960s turned into the 1970s, and it was heavily informed by the political environment of the time. Following recent legislation, suspects could now refuse to speak to the police unless a legal representative was present.

To liberals, this was a vital recognition of basic human rights. To those with more right-wing views, it was hampering cops from doing their job – typical of the social changes of the time that seemed to care more about the criminals than the victims.

The character of Harry Callahan played to the right-wing backlash. Callahan wasn't interested in criminals' rights, he just wanted to catch the bad guys. Faced in the script with a sadistic killer who was actively gaming the rules and regulations to stay free and keep on killing, Callahan went rogue and got the job done – his way.

After Sinatra passed on the script, John Wayne was approached. He turned it down, allegedly, because he found out that he wasn't first choice – and there's no way "the Duke" was going to take Sinatra's seconds.

George C. Scott, Robert Mitchum, Burt Lancaster and Steve McQueen also decided against the project before the script finally landed with Paul Newman. The character of Callahan was simply too right-wing for Newman's sensibilities so he turned the project down as well, but helpfully suggested that Clint Eastwood might be a match.

Eastwood agreed, but with one important proviso. The script had been rewritten several times – with the storyline increasingly softened – as the producers tried to attract an A-list star. The extreme behaviour of Callahan had been reined in, and the film had become less focused on his personal quest. Eastwood insisted on a reversion to the original storyline. He wanted the simple, brutal original tale of a cop going rogue reinstated.

In the final film, retitled *Dirty Harry*, the killer Scorpio is a motiveless sadist without a conscience. Everything possible is done to justify Callahan's decisions and actions.

Callahan's "just get it done" behaviour is epitomised in the iconic film moment when he decides he really can't be bothered to arrest a criminal who might later exploit a clever legal loophole to avoid justice. Instead, Callahan taunts Scorpio into reaching for a gun, so that he can simply kill him. You probably know the line.

> I know what you're thinking. "Did he fire six shots or only five?" Well, to tell you the truth, in all this excitement I kind of lost track myself. But being as this is a .44 Magnum, the most powerful handgun in the world, and would blow your head clean off, you've got to ask yourself one question: "Do I feel lucky?" Well, do ya, punk?

The audience at this point knows that Callahan has used this line before; and we know that he counts his bullets very carefully indeed. He knows exactly what will happen if Scorpio reaches for his gun.

Scorpio makes a move, and Callahan kills him. Luck had nothing to do with it.

Thanks, in part, to this moment, the "rogue cop" idea has since become one of the most popular devices of films and TV shows. As an audience we know that the moment the cop is asked by a superior to hand in their badge and gun is the moment the real action will begin. No longer constrained by the "red tape" of their job, the hero will now get results.

Why is this such a popular trope? We would not condone such extreme behaviour in real life, and most of us will never encounter such moments anyway. So why does the idea continue to fascinate us?

Surely it appeals to a mass audience because it resonates with a rogue element inside all of us. When we're faced with rules and regulations, a part of us just wants to cut through all that "nonsense" and get the job done.

The rogue cop appeals to this side of us.

So, as I present here a formal six-step process for good storytelling in business, I know that it will be received with mixed emotions. On the one hand, great – here is a simple process that will allow you to improve your business storytelling in all platforms and formats. But on the other hand, that part of you that identifies with the rogue cops doesn't really want to be hemmed in by a series of rules and regulations. You just want to allow your creativity to run free. Couldn't you just fire up PowerPoint, offer up a quick incantation to the Muses and head straight for "the flow state", from which all your best ideas emerge?

Well, you *could*. And maybe sometimes you'll come up with great results. But often you won't. What this six-step process offers is *repeatable* magic. Every presentation and document you create will be better.

But is it just a layer of additional work? No, the work you do at an early stage in using the SUPERB process to structure your writing is work that will be saved later on. There will be less need for editing, less time staring at a blank screen trying to work out where a particular slide goes, less time debating with colleagues how to cut down from 100 slides to the 30 you're supposed to have, and less angst as you have to deal with brutal feedback from stakeholders because they can't work out what you're trying to say.

How storytelling takes shape at work

Our first step is to understand how the stages of a story from films, TV or novels that we have discussed in the previous chapters translate into the work environment.

Importantly, this is not about telling anecdotes about your childhood or about something interesting you saw on the way into the office to busy, time-pressed colleagues who frankly would rather get to the point. It's about using the powerful elements of storytelling to construct equally powerful workplace communications.

The table below shows clearly how we can create equivalents to the storytelling elements we met in Chapter 2 in our work communications to deliver the same emotional effect.

The "What happens in a good story" column shows the stages of a conventional story. The next column outlines what the equivalent for this would be in a work situation. And the right-hand column introduces the stages of the SUPERB process that will bring these to life.

Act	What happens in a good story	What needs to happen in a successful workplace communication	The steps of the SUPERB process that accomplish this
One	The audience is made to identify strongly with the hero	The audience must be made to align with the creator (the writer, if a document; the speaker, if a presentation)	*Shared experiences*
	The audience understands what quest the hero is on and what their destination is	The audience must understand what success looks like – what the ultimate benefits of agreeing with the creator will be	*Ultimate triumph*
Two	The hero meets a major challenge and decides to take it on	The audience must be clear on what challenges lie ahead	*Problem definition*
	The hero successfully overcomes the challenge	The audience must be clear on how the creator proposes to deal with these challenges	*Explore options ...*
	The hero faces successive, more difficult challenges and overcomes them, usually with the help of allies	The audience must feel that the challenges *they* see ahead are recognised and acknowledged	*... and objections*

Three	To prepare to overcome the hardest challenge the hero has to see themselves and/or the world in a new way	The audience must be given a vivid understanding of the realities of the situation, including insights into how things are changing	*Real*
	The hero succeeds	The audience must be satisfied that they have understood and welcome the benefits of the proposal	*Best of both worlds*

Throughout this chapter, I will assume that the task is to write a presentation where we are trying to sell in a new idea to an audience – a "pitch". There are four reasons for this.

1. It will be simpler and clearer to explain the SUPERB process using one specific work-related task. The ways in which the SUPERB process can be applied to other tasks (other forms of presentations, documents, emails, meetings) are outlined in Chapter 7.

2. A pitch is one of the most obvious examples of the basic task of trying to persuade someone to do something, so offers a very clear way of discussing exactly what each stage of the SUPERB process is designed to achieve.

3. There is a Zen saying: "When you climb a mountain, begin at the top." Pitches are among the toughest, most high-pressure business situations, where a lot of money (and career progression) can be riding on the ability of the presenter(s) to tell a compelling story. So let's begin by showing how the SUPERB process can deal with the toughest task. After that, everything else will be (relatively) easy.

4. Using a pitch as our initial example is helpful because it allows us to deal with another obstacle that gets in the way of storytelling; the desire to win. There is a

natural tendency when pitching to talk about "winning" a pitch. This is unhelpful language, and calling it out will underline even more strongly that what all our communication needs to do is not to win an argument but to build an emotional connection.

If you try to "win a pitch" you have reduced your audience to the role of two-dimensional switches. They are either "on" or "off". They either say "yes" or "no". If they choose us, you will like them and admire their extraordinary perspicacity and understanding of business. If they choose some other firm, you will hate them and declare that they are idiots who just don't get it.

Who would want to be reduced to the role of a switch? If you bring this mindset to a pitch you are already alienating your audience. You are distancing yourself from them emotionally instead of bringing them closer. The more you try to "win", the more likely you are to lose.

You should not try to "win" a pitch. You should try to build a relationship.

That's what a successful pitch is. It's not a victory for you. It's the beginning of a relationship between you and the customer.

In everything that follows, remember that telling a story – in any format – is about building a relationship.

Inside the SUPERB storytelling model

The six-step SUPERB storytelling model looks like this:

Shared experiences
Ultimate triumph
Problem definition
Explore options and objections
Real
Best of both worlds

Shared experiences

In conventional storytelling, the writer has to manage the tricky task of making the audience identify with the hero of their story. They do this with techniques like Save the Cat.

In work settings, you're lucky. You don't have to do anything quite as complicated as this. But you have to do something *like* it. You need to create a similar sense of alignment. Wherever possible the audience will be the hero of the story, and your task is therefore simply to make sure that they feel that you are aligned with them.

As early as possible, you need to create a feeling that you agree with each other, that you're coming from a similar place and have similar aims. The relationship expert John Gottman once said: "The way a discussion starts determines the way it will end." This is true in friendships and romantic relationships, and it's true in work meetings; a communication that begins in a place of agreement is more likely to remain in agreement and, crucially, end in agreement.

The equivalent of Save the Cat is to use *Shared Experiences* – starting your story with something that you share with your audience, something that you can all agree on, a moment that aligns you with them. This can be complex: illustrating how your business faces the same challenges as your prospect's business, showing the board that your department's needs are aligned with their overall vision. Or it can be incredibly simple.

Exactly how simple is illustrated by Sir Ken Robinson's TED talk "Do schools kill creativity?". Robinson's talk grew to become the most watched TED talk of all time, so that a blog on the TED website referred to him as "the sneezing baby panda of the TED ecosystem" – a reference to a hugely popular (and very cute) viral video.[1]

But how did this talk win such a following? The speaker

wasn't famous (before the TED talk); the subject (though important) wasn't one that would naturally appeal to a wide audience; and the title wasn't remotely "click-baity".

Here, for comparison, are the titles of some other popular TED talk titles:

How great leaders inspire action

How to speak so that people want to listen

10 ways to have a better conversation

What makes a good life? Lessons from the longest study on happiness

How to spot a liar

How to make stress your friend

The happy secret to better work

All of these are surely more likely to get the casual YouTube watcher to click on "play" than "Do schools kill creativity?". And yet Robinson's talk trounces them all. What makes it so popular?

It's a word-of-mouth phenomenon. Everyone who watches it recommends it to others. And this happens because Robinson was a wonderful communicator. He was, in particular, brilliant at building a relationship almost instantly with a room full of strangers. The first few seconds of "Do schools kill creativity?" is a masterclass.

Here's the opening few seconds:

"Good morning. How are you?
    "It's been great, hasn't it? I've been blown away by the whole thing. In fact, I'm leaving.

"There have been three themes, haven't there, running through the conference, which are relevant to what I want to talk about.

"One is the extraordinary evidence of human creativity in all of the presentations that we've had and in all of the people here ..."

That's all he needs. Just those few sentences. Compare it with most TED talks and you'll note that it is extraordinarily low-key. It doesn't exactly jump off the page. It almost looks as though nothing is really happening. But in fact, a great deal is happening.

Watch it again (or re-read it) and note how many methods he has used, in those few words, to build a relationship with his audience.

It starts with a genuine, warm, human gesture of alignment: "How are you?"

This hardly seems like anything at all. He's just chatting. We all say that, don't we? But watch a few more TED talks, and you'll see that most speakers *don't* do it. And how strange is that? Why do so many public speakers and presenters omit to say a simple greeting?

And why is this simple greeting so important? Because in those three words "How are you?", Robinson has set the tone for everything that follows. Now he isn't talking *at* the audience. He's talking *with* them. He's not giving a speech. They're having a conversation.

Note how conversational the next lines are.

"It's been great, hasn't it?"

"There have been three themes, haven't there?"

In these two questions, Robinson has completed a transition. He's no longer an entirely separate person giving a speech to a group of other separate people; he has established himself as a member of the audience sharing the experience of the day together with the rest of the audience.

The first question invites the answer "Yes" – creating a *shared experience* and a point of agreement. By the time he gets to the second question, Robinson has won the audience over so completely that you find yourself thinking "Yes" when he says there have been three themes even though you weren't at the conference and you don't yet know what themes he is about to call out. How has he done this? By beginning with *shared experiences* and by beginning in a place of agreement.

If we agree with someone about one thing, we tend to think that we will agree with them about other things too.

We all know this phenomenon. If you meet someone at a party and you find that their favourite film is *your* favourite film, you immediately assume that you will have other things in common too.

To create alignment between yourself and your audience, take advantage of this by creating a clear moment of agreement right at the beginning. In this way you begin to evolve in the eyes of your audience from "someone presenting to me" into "someone who I tend to agree with about things".

Robinson does more than this. In the space of these few lines, he also lightens the mood – and again brings his own status level with the audience – through a self-deprecatory joke:

"I'm leaving."

And then he again raises the status of the audience with some basic flattery.

Note in particular how different his approach is from other TED talk speakers and other presenters you may have seen.

He doesn't try to dominate or own the space.

He doesn't begin with an anecdote about himself.

He starts a conversation not a speech.

He identifies himself with the audience, not separate from it.

He creates immediate agreement, not surprise or intrigue.

The "Do schools kill creativity?" opening is such a good example of the *shared experiences* technique *because there is no technique on show*. Robinson is so relentlessly low-key and casual that I don't think he consciously employs a "presentation technique" at any point. I suspect that Robinson was simply a genuinely kind and empathetic person who naturally communicated in this way. But this quiet, unassuming approach shows how natural and simple *shared experiences* can be.

But the technique can also be deep and complex. I once worked with an ad agency that was re-pitching for a car company account. It had held the account for over a decade and, frankly, its levels of client service had started to slip.

The agency management admitted that they had taken their eye off the ball. They promised to do better in future. But why should the client believe them? Or, more importantly, reappoint them?

The car company's marketing strategy revolved around a complete reinvention of its range. It would be built on new platforms promising better quality and reliability than in the past (when its reputation had been less than great). The agency team began their re-pitch presentation by discussing this marketing strategy, discussing in positive terms the way the car company was asking for a new relationship with its customers that was based on the superior new models going forward, not the less good models of the past.

Having got the client nodding along in agreement, the agency team switched tack to discuss the analogous situation that they were in: promising a better future, and asking the client to judge them on this, not on their past record.

Having already agreed that they themselves expected to be judged on future promises not past track record, the client could hardly now say that they could not possibly do the same for the agency.

The *shared experiences* technique had been used to get a moment of agreement that the slate could be wiped clean. The shared experience was: our company is in exactly the same situation as your company, and we are making the same request of you that you are making of your customers. For the rest of the pitch, the agency was no longer on the back foot. And it won.

You will not always be able to come up with such a closely matched shared experience, but the nature of business means that you can often locate an "our company is facing the same challenges as your company" moment.

And when this is not possible, your default option to create alignment is a series of "enrolling questions" – questions to which the answer is "Yes". Sir Ken Robinson used a couple, didn't he?

SUPERB step	Description	Objective
Shared experiences	Call-backs to a shared moment, and/or positive things that we can all agree on	Creates *alignment* between yourself and your audience

Ultimate triumph

When you're reading a novel or watching a film, you need to know what the story is *about*. To recall David Mamet's description, you need to know "what the hero is trying to get". In a heist film, the gang is trying to get away with the money. In an Avengers film, the superheroes are trying to save the Universe. In a romcom, the boy/girl is trying to get the girl/boy.

To retain your attention the writer needs to make sure that you know what the quest is. Similarly, when presenting you need to make sure that your audience knows what the quest you're discussing is, and how they will know when the quest has been achieved.

If the audience is the hero of your story, what are they trying to get? What is their quest? This is the *ultimate triumph*.

In a pitch the *ultimate triumph* ought to be fairly obvious. There will have been a brief that explains what the client wants, and perhaps you have built on the brief to offer something more.

But it's extraordinary how often the team that is pitching will either ignore the brief, offer something different, or – even when delivering what is wanted – wait until the last slide to reveal that this is the case. You need to avoid all these errors. An absolute focus on "what the hero is trying to get" makes for a great presentation. And you need to establish "what they are trying to get" as soon as possible.

One of the biggest mistakes that people make in writing or presenting is giving lots of context before getting to their main point – setting things up, or "showing their working". Finally, *eventually*, there is a "benefits slide" – which contains the information that the audience has been waiting for all along. This gradual build makes perfect sense to the creator, but it alienates an audience. Context isn't interesting unless people know what it's the context *to*.

To create a powerful story, you must establish the *ultimate triumph* very early. If the audience don't know the aim of the quest, they won't come on the journey. If they don't know what's in it for them, they won't listen.

In a pitch, then, the *ultimate triumph* is what the audience will get if they choose to work with you. In a presentation to internal stakeholders, it's the advantage to the audience of doing what you are asking them to do. In a review of the year's activity, it could be the one standout indicator which will inform the next year's strategy. In an analysis of a project, it could be the most successful outcome of the project, or it could be the learning that will make the next project better (depending on your audience – and what matters to them).

SUPERB step	Description	Objective
Ultimate triumph	The potential benefits to your audience of the subject you are discussing	Creates *interest* in what you are saying

Problem definition

In this step and the one that follows – *Explore options and objections* – the SUPERB process actively mirrors the conflict/resolution framework of the Hollywood model, based on the hero's journey, which was covered in detail in Chapter 2.

Imagine someone pitching these films to a Hollywood studio.

Policeman John McClane wants to reconcile with his estranged wife. So he meets her at a party and they get back together.

A shark is terrorising a seaside town. So some expert shark-hunters quickly kill the shark before it can do any harm.

A fish called Marlon tells his son Nemo that the ocean is a very dangerous place. So Nemo sensibly stays close to his dad.

There's a big iceberg heading for a ship. So the ship steers out of the way.

Ridiculous, right? In these guises, *Die Hard*, *Jaws*, *Finding Nemo* and *Titanic* would never have got made. No one would watch those films. No one would care.

Everyone knows that a story where everything progresses smoothly isn't a story. There have to be challenges, and they have to be difficult. And yet, again and again, people try to write a business story in which everything progresses smoothly, in which absolutely nothing goes wrong.

Their motives are understandable. They don't want to admit that their organisation faces problems, or that they themselves may struggle with certain challenges. But if you don't admit and identify the challenges (even if this feels uncomfortable) you really don't have a story.

In a pitch the client has (hopefully) already identified – and therefore admitted to – the problem. This problem needs to be reflected back to them as part of your ongoing demonstration that you are telling their story, not your story. If you jump straight to your great offering without discussing their problem, then they will suspect that you don't care about their problems, and you are not really that interested in solving them – merely in selling your products or services and making money out of them.

In internal presentations you may meet greater resistance to admitting that a problem exists – or disagreement about what the nature of the problem is. Wherever possible, therefore, you need to engage your audience in a diagnostic session before you write your presentation. You may meet obstacles here (they don't have time, or they're just not interested) but most people get the point: that if you can talk to them about their issue first, your presentation will be more relevant to them and more likely to offer them what they need.

If all this emphasis on problems is starting to sound negative, it really isn't, because you're not just identifying problems: you're going to go on to overcome them.

SUPERB step	Description	Objective
Problem definition	Identification and analysis of the challenges	Creates *engagement* with your point

Explore options and objections

You want to overcome challenges. But you don't want to do that too easily. You don't want to jump too quickly to the right answer. Before you offer your solution, you need to explore some other options.

Why do this?

First, exploring different possible solutions makes for a stronger story. If the first thing you think of is the answer, the challenge can't have been that difficult. And if the challenge isn't difficult, the story isn't strong.

Second, a pitch is not a game show. There isn't one perfect right answer that wins you the prize money. In almost all work situations, things are a little more nuanced than that. You may need to compare and contrast several options before you find the one that, on balance, is the best.

Third, this approach also shows that you are prepared to put in some hard work on behalf of the audience. It is further evidence that you care about them.

And finally, in a pitch, this approach allows you to subtly

criticise the approaches you think your rival companies might offer.

The best approach is essentially to follow what you might term "the Goldilocks model": too hot, too cold, just right.

This model was exemplified in a pitch for a bank that I consulted on where the brief was to recruit new current account holders. The agency first talked about targeting a young demographic because they were more likely to switch, but they were also more likely to switch *out* of the bank again. Then they explored targeting an older demographic because they had more money, but they were resistant to switching so would prove prohibitively expensive to recruit. Finally, the agency recommended targeting a demographic in the middle – they were easier/cheaper to recruit than the older group, and easier to keep hold of than the younger group, so their lifetime customer value to the bank would be the greatest of the three groups.

Using more than three options gets too complex, but the "too hot, too cold, just right" Goldilocks approach is familiar and easily understood by the audience.

In the SUPERB model you may sometimes want to repeat the *problem definition* and *explore options* steps for each of a series of challenges. The structure should be challenge, solution, challenge, solution, challenge, solution rather than listing all the challenges first and then offering all the solutions.

This allows you to mirror the hero's journey storytelling structure more accurately, and also ensures that you don't spend too much time discussing challenges without offering an upside. If you spend too much time talking about problems before moving on to offer solutions, you may start to build uncertainty and doubt in your audience. Confronting challenges is vital. Wallowing in them for extended periods of time is not a good idea.

Crucially, in the SUPERB model even when you present your preferred option, you don't present it as the perfect answer.

This is simply not realistic. Nothing in business is perfect. Any solution you recommend is likely to have a few flaws. And your audience is likely to be thinking about these. Which is why you have to *explore objections*.

Although the audience may be pondering some objections to your solution, it is possible that they won't raise these objections at the time. Even if you remember to leave time for questions, even if you actively encourage the audience's participation, some people just don't like to speak up. Some are shy. Some want to avoid the possibility of conflict. They will instead mull over what they think is wrong with your pitch in their head, and only discuss it with the rest of their team after you've gone. At which point you have no time to push back or to defend your position.

Because you can't rely on them to raise possible objections, you have to do it for them. Rather than allow their objections to live in their inner monologue, where they will grow and fester, you must bring them out into the open by discussing them yourself.

In this way your audience feels heard (even though you're doing the talking), and you again demonstrate that you care about them, by providing the workarounds to any possible problems with your solution.

It's tempting to wonder if it wouldn't be better to just shut up and hope you "get away with it". But it wouldn't be, because you won't. Their objections will surface later. In any communication – and particularly in a pitch – the audience's inner monologue is one of your biggest problems. You must not allow their potential objections to reside there.

SUPERB step	Description	Objective
Explore options and objections	Look at several solutions. Explain your choice. Show possible problems and workarounds	Creates a sense of mutual *discovery* between you and your audience

Real

In novels, films and plays, the creators can leave some things to the audience's imagination. They can work on the assumption that their audience is expecting to be entertained and will do a bit of extra work to negotiate the intricacies of their plot. In the workplace you can't afford to be so subtle. Perhaps your audience will give you their undivided attention for the entire length of your presentation and catch every word and every meaning, but it's taking a big risk to assume that this is going to happen.

Instead, you must make everything absolutely clear. You must make everything you say or write seem as real as possible. You must bring your solution vividly to life.

Blake Snyder, author of *Save the Cat!*, says: "The 'who' is our way in." If a communication stays in the world of strategy, data and concepts, it can be hard for the audience to take in. So you need to explain the key ideas in your pitch using the experiences of individual people.

Wherever possible, root what you are discussing in one person's life. For example:

If you are proposing a new process, show how will it affect the day or week of one individual.

If you are pitching a marketing campaign, show how it will be experienced by one consumer.

If you are selling a B2B service, show how it will change the life of the end user.

If you are asking for help on a project, show exactly what the commitment will be for an audience member.

If you are describing the benefits of something, make it clear what the tangible "quick wins" will be for an audience member.

If you are discussing cultural change, break it down into precise changed behaviours for people in specific roles.

Abstract concepts don't play well in a story. Vivid, graspable reality does.

SUPERB step	Description	Objective
Real	Bring your solution vividly to life. Ideally through the actual experience of one individual	Creates real *understanding* of your point

Best of both worlds

How does your story end?

It ends with the *ultimate triumph* that you promised at the beginning of the story successfully attained. You have been through the problems, explored ways of tackling them, and finally prevailed. Of course, you haven't done the work yet. But you've outlined the complete path to the end of the quest. You promised them that you would shave 10% off costs, and now you've shown them exactly how it will be done. You told them that you can successfully introduce the new process by the end of the year, and now you've shown them exactly how you'll achieve that.

Unfortunately, it's not quite that simple. You can give a

client or stakeholder exactly what they asked for and still lose the pitch. It's exasperating, but it's true. There are several possible reasons for this, but one of the most common reasons – and one of the easiest to remedy once you know about it – is that the client doesn't hear the benefit that you are expressing because you are expressing it in a language with which they are not comfortable.

One of the challenges in any form of communication is understanding your audience well enough to know how they will react. In some instances, you may know them well and have a fair idea of how they will respond; in other cases, they may be completely unknown to you. You may be dealing with one individual, who you can research thoroughly; or you may be reaching out to a large, disparate group, all of whom have very different attitudes and personalities. How can you create a piece of communications that is suited to them all?

Of course, you can't do this completely. But there is one personality trait that you *must* acknowledge in the conclusion of your presentation if you want to maximise your chances of success.

This trait will define how an individual responds to the conclusion of your story. There are different ways of discussing it, but perhaps the most accessible and usable comes from the world of neurolinguistic programming, where some practitioners divide people into "towards" and "away from" categories.[2]

As the name suggests, "towards" people are motivated by an exciting future that they wish to move *towards*. "Away from" people are motivated by *avoiding* problems and dangers that they want to stay away from.

A simple example: ask a "towards" person about work/life balance and they may say: "I just want to get home in time to read my kids a bedtime story". In making essentially the same point (I want a good work/life balance) an "away from" person would say something more like: "If I don't leave at 5.30 at least a couple of days a week, my stress levels go through the roof." The former looks towards a positive, fun goal. The latter seeks to avoid a negative problem. They see exactly the same situation (and the same goal) from precisely the opposite perspective.

Their use of language is a vital clue to their personality and what motivates them. It means, unfortunately, that the very same words and phrases that attract the "towards" people in your audience can repel the "away froms".

If your presentation talks relentlessly about a bright, shiny, innovative solution you will be scoring points with "towards" people but actively alienating "away froms", who will be wondering what fresh hell this new plan of yours will unleash on their working day. If you talk exclusively about problem-solving and banishing inefficiencies the "away froms" will like you but the "towards" crowd will be wondering how soon they will be able to leave the room and put some distance between themselves and your gloomy worldview.

If you are presenting to someone you know, you may well be able to determine which group they belong to, in which case you can use the appropriate language in your conclusion.

However, if you are presenting to someone you don't know well, or to a group of people which might feature both "towards" and "away from" individuals, then you have to offer them the *best of both worlds*.

You must conclude your story with a happy outcome for both. You have to promise just enough (but not too many) exciting "towards" benefits and just enough (but not too much) safety and security.

SUPERB step	Description	Objective
Best of both worlds	Give an exciting vision of the future for "towards" people, and a safe one for "away from" people	Creates *agreement* and buy-in with your proposal

*

For the sake of simplicity, the SUPERB model has been introduced in this chapter as it would be used in a pitch. But it's much more versatile than that. In the next two chapters you will see how it can be used in other presentations, when working with data, in documents and emails – and also as a way of structuring important meetings.

Before you move on, here is a handy reference of the whole model.

The complete SUPERB model

Step	Description	Objective
Shared experiences	Call-backs to a shared moment, and/or positive things that we can all agree on	Creates *alignment* between yourself and your audience
Ultimate triumph	The potential benefits to your audience of the subject you are discussing	Creates *interest* in what you are saying
Problem definition	Identification and analysis of the challenges	Creates *engagement* with your point
Explore options and objections	Look at several solutions. Explain your choice. Show possible problems and workarounds	Creates a sense of mutual *discovery* between you and your audience
Real	Bring your solution vividly to life. Ideally through the actual experience of one individual	Creates real *understanding* of your point

| Best of both worlds | Give an exciting vision of the future for "towards" people, and a safe one for "away from" people | Creates *agreement* and buy-in with your proposal |

6

Storytelling with data

**How to unlock the stories that lie in the data; how
the SUPERB model brings data stories to life; and
why you should never, ever use a pie chart**

It's the summer of 2009, and Stanley A. McChrystal, recently
appointed to lead all US forces in Afghanistan, is sitting through
a PowerPoint presentation in Kabul. It's one of about fifteen
PowerPoint presentations that the general has to sit through
every week in his new role.

At one point a slide appears which has been designed to
portray the complexity of US strategy in Afghanistan at the
time. It features 13 headings such as "Population conditions
and beliefs", "Tribal governance", "Popular support" and
"Narcotics".

In between these loosely scattered headings are close
to a hundred subheadings such as "Coalition knowledge
and understanding of social structures", "Cultural erosion/
displacement" and "Transparency of government processes
and investments". These are all joined together with a veritable
spaghetti of arrows. And all the above is colour-coded into
eight different groupings.

It's a challenging read, to say the least. And General

McChrystal, famous for his outspokenness, sums up the feeling in the room when he declares: "When we understand that slide, we will have won the war."

His comment is funny, but it's not accurate. Understanding that slide would not lead to winning the war. Understanding it would not lead to anything. All the slide contains is information and you could absorb all that information and still have no idea what to do next.

Most of us don't have to fight wars. But we are often presented with similarly complex and unhelpful PowerPoint slides and impenetrable documents. Whenever somebody who has a lot of information (or, as we prefer to refer to it these days, data) needs to convey that information or data to another person or group of people, there's a good chance that equally baffling content will be presented.

Data can tell a powerful story – if you let it

Data sits at the heart of more and more organisations, and, increasingly, executives look to data to guide both long-term strategies and tactical decisions. However, it is also extremely common for organisations to report that they are not seeing the benefits that they initially expected from the increasing amounts and granularity of data now available to them. There may be several reasons for this, but one of the key reasons is the problems that occur at work when data-literate people communicate to non-data-literate people.

To get the most from data, an organisation has first to establish what the data *means*, and then to establish its *value*. In most cases, for this journey from data to meaning to value to be completed successfully, specialists have to talk to generalists and this communication can often be less than optimal.

This is frustrating because data really should enhance a

story. Indeed, data can be a powerful creator of stories, the tool that reveals the twists and turns in a market or an organisation that form the basis of stories. But anyone who has sat through a presentation or struggled through a report loaded with complex and baffling charts and tables might find this hard to believe.

So what goes wrong?

Without wanting to fall prey to stereotypes, there can be a tendency for those who work with lots of data to be more analytical people, some of whom may be less naturally inclined to believe that storytelling is a powerful way to communicate. After all, one of the central ideas that explains why storytelling is important (as we saw in Chapter 1) is the fact that people make decisions emotionally, not for logical reasons. We like to *think* we make decisions for logical reasons, and the logical part of our brain goes to some efforts to make it seem as though this is true.

People who spend their days working with data can hold quite tightly to the idea that decisions at work are overwhelmingly made for logical, data-driven reasons, and therefore can be quite resistant to the idea that they will communicate more powerfully by taking an *emotional* storytelling approach. Also, they may lack confidence in their own ability to tell stories and communicate on an emotional level, making it feel safer for them to simply hide behind the charts. Lots of charts. Lots and lots and lots of charts.

By staying in their comfort zone, and by communicating in a way that makes sense to them, they unfortunately fail to communicate in a way that truly reaches their audiences. They miss out on learning and developing a valuable skill. Their audiences are often bored, and the value that lies hidden in the data sadly *stays* hidden in the data – to the detriment of everyone.

The SUPERB model can be particularly helpful in creating

data-based stories, in part because it allows people to see storytelling almost as an engineering process rather than an arty or creative one. At the same time the model gives clear signals in how to convert data into story.

When I coach teams of data specialists, I find that the elements of the SUPERB process that particularly resonate with them are:

This isn't about them. They don't have to have natural storytelling skills – and they don't have to talk about themselves.

This isn't a "creative" task. Of course, they are creating something, but they're not doing this via brainstorms and stretch sessions.

There is a clear process to follow, and the closer you follow the process the more successful your results will tend to be.

From data to meaning to value

The data itself may speak clearly to the person who has run the numbers and to the person creating the presentation or document but it won't speak clearly to a non-data-literate audience. For good data-based communication to a generalist audience to take place, the data must be transformed first into meaning and then into value, and this important transformation has to occur *before* you can even begin to build your story.

Not only are many data-literate people not trained in storytelling, but some are not even trained in the basic skill of translating data into meaning; they work on the assumption that the job of finding the meaning lies with their audience. But this task can often be beyond a non-data-literate audience.

Why do I keep repeating this inelegant phrase "non-data-literate audience"? Because it is highly likely that the most powerful people in the audience – the key decision-makers – will be those who have had little training in understanding data and equally little inclination to do the work necessary to interpret charts and understand the true meaning of the figures. Even if they did at some point have that skill, they may well have spent many years being spoon-fed carefully curated information in one-pagers and executive summaries. As far as they are concerned, someone else is supposed to decode the information for them.

And even when the presentation is not being given to someone who has the status and privilege to begin all conversations by abruptly stating: "Just give me the top line", there is a wider issue that applies to all audiences:

If it's hard to read, it's hard to do.

This idea originates in research by Hyunjin Song and Norbert Schwarz at the University of Michigan, who found that:

people misread the difficulty of processing instructions as indicative of the difficulty of executing the behaviour, and that this misperception has downstream effects on their willingness to engage in that behaviour.[1]

This research shows that when people are confronted by information that is hard to decode, they assume that the task it describes will also be hard to do. So, for example, if the instructions for a new piece of tech are impenetrable, we tend to assume that the tech itself will be equally un-user-friendly. Faced with charts and tables that look as though they are going to take a lot of work to read, the audience will tend to assume that the information contained in the charts and tables will also be hard to understand, and that any tasks that might need to be done as a result of the information presented will be hard to do.

Make your charts easy to read and people are more likely to both get your point and to agree with any recommendations you may go on to make.

There are three types of data-based presentation

Throughout this chapter, for clarity's sake, we will assume that the communication under discussion is a presentation – a PowerPoint deck. However, the same basic principles apply to a document or any other work that involves a lot of data.

Data-based presentations generally take one of three forms: Represent, Report or Recommend.

> *Represent*. The fundamental purpose of this kind of presentation is to explain (either to another company or to an internal stakeholder) what the data team does and how it does it. The brief is: "Tell us how you work" or "Take us through your capabilities."

> *Report*. Here, the purpose is to take the audience through a set of data. The brief is: "Bring us up to date on sales", "Take us through third quarter activity" or "Can we have a debrief on the recent research project?"

> *Recommend*. In this instance the purpose is to give an indication of what the data tells us. The brief is more pointed: "Did anything interesting come out of that consumer research?" or "What are our competitors doing and how should we react?"

However, a useful working hypothesis is that, in almost all cases, however the brief is presented, the audience would like an element of *Recommend*.

The brief "Tell us how you work" actually means "Tell us how you work, *and which bits of the work you do are particularly relevant to me and my company*". "Take us through your capabilities" means "Take us through your capabilities *and highlight the capabilities that could add value*". And "Bring us up to date on sales" means "Bring us up to date on sales *and please highlight any particularly exciting or alarming trends.*"

The data is not the hero of the story

One of the key skills in storytelling – thinking about your audience and starting where *they* are, not where *you* want to start – is even more true when data comes into the picture.

Remember that your task is not to communicate your work: it is to communicate the value of the work to the audience. Nobody wants you to show all your workings.

This is true in most cases. There may be some occasions when someone is expressly asked to show a complete set of research – a genuine *Report*, not *Recommend* brief. But these are rare. In most cases, the audience wants you to edit things down. The tendency not to do this – to show all the data – comes either from a desire to show how hard somebody has worked or how much effort a particular department has put in, to prove that the brief and scope of work have been fully understood, or in the paranoid belief that if something goes wrong in the future you might be blamed for the whole fiasco because you failed to show the one crucial figure that would have changed everything.

You can usually satisfy all these criteria by having a "leave-behind" appendix which contains all the data, shown in every

Best Story Wins

conceivable combination, which can be an optional read rather than something that everyone is forced to sit through.

When editing, keep reminding yourself that just as you are not the hero, the data isn't the hero either. The audience is still the hero. The data doesn't have to show up in its entirety.

Before you tell the story, find the value

It's clear that one reason why data-based communication can sometimes be so difficult to absorb and understand is that what's really taking place is simply a lengthy download of all the data available, without any attempt made to decide what's important.

To avoid this, you can employ the four-stage SAFE process before you embark on the SUPERB storytelling process.

Source the data

Analyse the data to find out what it means for your audience

Find the one fact, figure or insight that holds the most value for your audience

Eliminate everything that doesn't hold meaning or value for your audience

By front-loading the crucial work of finding the value in the data, the subsequent creation of the story becomes much easier.

Source the data

This stage should be fairly self-explanatory. You run the numbers or find the already available data and compile it.

130

Analyse the data to find out what it means for your audience

It's not enough to just put the data in front of your audience. You have to do the work upfront to decide what in this data holds meaning for your audience. To do that, you have to understand who your audience is, and what matters to them. If the presentation is to an internal audience or a regular client or customer, hopefully you will already know this or can pick the brains of a colleague who does.

If the audience is a new external prospect, for example, you may have been given a clear brief which should help you understand what has meaning and what has value for them. But we all know only too well that we are often tasked with projects with only the vaguest of briefs. If this is the case, there is no substitute for taking the time to research your audience: what they do, what they need, what they think, what they feel.

Do this by talking to them, if that's possible; talking to colleagues of yours who have worked with them before. Or, if all direct human routes are closed to you, then it's time for some online digging. Who is this company? What does it do? What matters to the company? Who are its customers and what matters to *them*? Who are the people who are going to be in the room listening to you? What have they said in public before?

Look at the company's customer-facing website, its website, LinkedIn, YouTube and other social media. Having absorbed the language and the online activity of the individuals, interrogate the data to find the elements that are most likely to resonate with them. (While you are doing this, also be on the lookout for any potential *shared experiences* – areas where your company is aligned with theirs or faces similar challenges.)

Find the one fact, figure or insight that holds the most value for your audience

Having identified those key areas that hold meaning for our audience – all of which should survive into your story – the next task is to identify the one key nugget that holds the most value. Sometimes this will be obvious; sometimes it's a judgement call. But it's a call you have to make in order to have a strong story.

Eliminate everything that doesn't hold meaning or value for your audience

Having filtered the data twice – first to find the areas that have meaning for your audience and then once more to find the one area with the most value – the next task is to decide what to do with all the rest. Unless you have been expressly briefed to present everything, try to remove as much of the rest of the data as possible.

Some people find this very difficult to do. It helps to involve a "naïve witness" (a colleague not involved in the task) to bounce ideas off, and offer you support in making the decision to drop material at this stage. If you find you cannot leave anything out then use the back-up option of an appendix, and shunt most of the data there so that it doesn't detract from the value of your main story.

Applying the SUPERB process to a data story

Having carried out this preliminary work, you can now start building your story using the SUPERB process in much the same way as in Chapter 5. If you need a refresher on the basics of the SUPERB process, look back over that chapter; what follows here is the *additional* work you need to do when a story leans heavily on data. The largest amount of additional work is needed in the *real* stage, because bringing data vividly to life brings its own unique challenges.

Shared experiences

When telling a data-heavy story to a general audience, even more care must be taken to "start where they are" – because if "where you are" is steeped in data, you can be sure they are somewhere else. So, the alignment with your audience offered by the *shared experiences* stage is absolutely crucial.

What are your shared experiences with the audiences? If you are talking to people in your own company, then the shared goals of your company, previous meetings you have had with these colleagues, or the well-known aspects of the company's culture can all be sources of shared experiences.

If you are talking to people from another company, the shared experiences can ideally be found in the brief. If they're not there, then you may well have encountered them while researching your audience during your preliminary SAFE work.

If you're struggling to find specific shared experiences, your back-up plan is to use enrolling questions – that is, questions to which the answer will inevitably be yes.

These can be questions that relate to current trends in their industry, which everyone would agree on. If you're still struggling, you can find your enrolling questions in the megatrends that effect the economy generally and the population widely.

These will very much depend on current events at the time you are writing the presentation, but to give you an idea, at the time of writing this book, the following would have done the job nicely.

Settling on a new way of working following the pandemic has proved problematic for many companies, hasn't it?

The cost of living is making things tough for your customers, isn't it?

There's so much data out there these days. Sometimes it can be hard to find the data that matters, can't it?

You're always simply looking to begin in a place of agreement.

Ultimate triumph

During the preliminary SAFE work, you have found the one fact, figure or insight that holds the most value for your audience. This is the *ultimate triumph*. It is crucial that you state this value to your audience clearly and very near the beginning of your communication.

In a *Represent* presentation, it will be a statement of the most significant value that your department or your work adds (or could add) to the audience.

In a *Report* presentation, it will be a statement of the most significant fact that the data reveals.

In a *Recommend* presentation, it will be a statement of the most important recommendation that you will make.

Achieving this clarity around one point is important to building the story structure; however, some people find it very uncomfortable to reduce so much work to one crucial point, as they see it. If this is you, there are ways to state the *ultimate triumph* while also retaining the idea that the overall picture is much more complex. For example:

We've got a lot to get through today, and honestly there are some complex issues to work through, but I think the key take out is that there is increasing evidence that we are significantly losing ground to the new disruptors in our market, and that addressing this has now become urgent.

Or:

As you requested, we are going to give you an overview of all the economic factors but if you only take one thing away from this presentation, it should be that the recent interest rate increases are significantly impacting our estimates of customer lifetime value.

Problem definition

In a data story, the *problem definition* centres on the challenges that you help your company or your clients deal with. As ever, with storytelling it's not about you. It's about the challenges that your stakeholders need you to help them with.

A clear exposition of the business challenge or problem under discussion shows that you have understood the brief, that you have conducted the right work, and helps create another moment of positive alignment with the audience.

Explore options and objections

The section allows you to communicate to the audience the benefits of your approach to tackling the brief. Why have you looked at one set of data and not another? Why have you analysed the data in one way and not another? Why are you showing them certain charts and not others?

The Goldilocks model works well here, taking the audience through the "too hot", "too cold" and "just right" approaches. For example:

We could have looked at X figures, but we didn't because they're not as current. We could have looked at Y figures, but we didn't because we do not think that they are robust enough. Instead we looked at Z figures, which we believe are the perfect combination of current, robust and meaningful to the problem we're addressing.

Similarly, you need to explore possible objections. What questions might the audience have about your approach? What might be worrying them? If they are not data specialists they may be particularly reluctant to raise the objections they have or ask their questions for fear of looking stupid ("Probably everyone else gets this except me"). Actively explore possible objections – and your justifications and workarounds while you can (and before they get stuck in your audience's inner monologue). For example:

You may be wondering why we have limited ourselves to looking at only these three regions. We have found in the past that they are the most representative. They are the quickest and most cost-effective way of getting a handle on the national picture without going to the added time and expense of commissioning nationwide research. Of course, if you feel the need for further reassurance, we could do that.

Real

The *real* phase is crucial in a data-heavy presentation, because it's likely that many of your audience are not specifically attuned to thinking in terms of data, charts and tables. Finding ways to bring the ideas that lie within the figures vividly to life for them is therefore vital. You can do this in four main ways.

1. Use storytelling headlines – and lean quite heavily on them.
2. Ask questions – and answer them.
3. Use only the simplest charts – and banish pie charts.
4. Remember that data has feelings too – or, at least, can inspire emotions.

Using storytelling headlines (as outlined in Chapter 4) is vital. The title of the chart should be relegated to the bottom of the slide. So, *underneath* the chart you can have: "Sales report nationwide by regions. Q4 2023 vs Q4, 2022" but the *headline* is: "Sales have increased 7% since the new pricing model was introduced".

But it's not enough simply to have a storytelling headline at the top of each slide. The headlines have to be used carefully. Use them to rethink the very nature of the presentation. Don't think that you are "presenting a chart". Instead, realise that you are telling the story in the headlines.

Make sure that *every* slide has a storytelling headline Then, as you move to a new slide, the storytelling headline must be the most prominent element. As it appears, say the storytelling headline out loud. This may seem like pointless duplication to you, but it's *important* duplication. If you are saying one thing while the audience is reading something else, at least one of those messages (and possibly both) will get lost.

It's helpful to use the technique of having a question as the transition between each pair of slides so that the question you ask as you finish discussing one slide is answered by the storytelling headline on the next slide. For example:

Headline A: Overall sales are up 7%

Presenter discusses Slide A, ending on Transitional Question to Slide B: But we said that growing the under-25s was important to us. How are we doing on that?

Headline B: Sales to 18–25-year-olds are up 12%

Headline A: 87% of employees say "I feel the company values me"

Presenter discusses Slide A, ending on Transitional Question to Slide B:

So that's the overall picture, but how are BAME employees feeling?

Headline B: Only 58% of BAME employees agree that "I feel the company values me"

In this way, you are carefully guiding the audience through the story, setting up each point before you deliver it.

Having written your storytelling headline, think very carefully: do you need a table or a chart at all? Do you even need any figures? Or can the storytelling headline carry the sense of the slide alone? In many cases, it can. I would urge you to resist the urge to put charts and tables and figures on every slide. They're not always needed.

However, if you feel there must be substantiation, first think about whether that can come simply in the form of one key figure without any need to have the whole chart or table. Can we simply say "73% of employees have already been trained in Agile working methods" without having a bar chart that looks at all the departments and shows different lines for which percentage in each department have been trained, with a squiggly line to show the mean or median percentage across departments? Is this level of detail necessary? Perhaps it is.

Maybe the key takeout is that one department is lagging behind all the others. But perhaps it isn't. Maybe all the audience cares about is that, overall, the company is on track with the retraining.

The right type of chart

If you're absolutely clear that you must have a chart, either because it's necessary or because you don't feel confident in presenting without it, then your next task is to choose the *right* type of chart.

Understanding the relative effectiveness of different chart types may seem a bit of a tangent for a book about storytelling, but it's not. The right chart type helps the story along. The wrong chart type brings it to a grinding halt.

You want people to follow the story you're telling in your headlines. The more time and effort it takes them to decode the charts and tables, the more they will get distracted from and forget the story. So choosing the chart type that most clearly and quickly conveys your point or justifies your headline is a vital element in telling a powerful story.

Anyone who has to present with data needs to understand how human beings read charts. We do this in the same way that we decode the world generally. We see first what stands out because of size, colour or oddness. We look for change and difference. We want to see only a very few elements, and then we try to make meaning from the elements we can see. If there is a lot of information, we are likely to shut down and refuse to take in any information or make any meaning.

There are some basic rules in how people read charts, and when presenting you mess with these at your peril.

Time moves from left to right.

Higher up means more or better.

If two elements share the same colour it means they are connected in some way.

If one element has a different or unique colour, it means that it is different in some way. And probably important.

If everything on the chart is the same size and colour, the implication is that none of it matters.

Charts that show visual change and difference where there is no change or difference in meaning are unhelpful. Charts that use differences in size, colour or shape without having a specific meaning for each are confusing. Charts that contain a lot of information are frankly an act of aggression towards the audience; they say: "I couldn't be bothered to sort this lot out – *you* do the work!"

Over the years much has been written about the best way to communicate with graphics. Time spent studying the classic works of Edward Tufte,[2] or the more recent output of Nancy Duarte[3] would be time well spent. At the very least, familiarise yourself with the Cleveland-McGill scale[4] – effectively a ranking for the clarity and accessibility of different chart types. This will ensure that you avoid those charts which are the hardest for non-data-literate people to understand.

The most important lesson that we can glean from the Cleveland-McGill scale is that the easiest chart for most people to understand is the common or garden bar chart. It's perhaps not surprising that people who work with charts all the time get bored of these and wish to do things that they think are more exciting. But they should resist the temptation. A "cool new chart" is almost certainly a chart that most people will struggle to understand.

If you can make your bar charts horizontal, rather than vertical, you have the added advantage that you can put the key to each bar alongside the bar itself. Make that horizontal too, so it can be read easily.

Charts that have the information positioned on a scale or represented by length are the simplest and easiest for us to understand. A slope or an angle (the classic hockey stick) is also relatively easy for us to get our heads round. But once you start using *areas* to convey your meaning, things get more difficult. Bubble charts are baffling. Heat maps are hard work. Three dimensions is one too many, so any form of volume chart should be resisted.

The noted statistician (and incidentally the coiner of the term "software") John Tukey put it bluntly: "There is no data that can be displayed in a pie chart, that cannot be displayed *better* in some other type of chart." And, by the way, the doughnut chart is even harder to make sense of than a pie chart. Basically, avoid all dessert-based visuals.

Bringing data to life

In the *real* stage, you want not just to make things clear, but also to make them vivid. You want to bring them to life. Ideally you will do this by finding the feelings hidden in the data. This may sound like a bit of a stretch, but it's not impossible. All you need to do is give yourself permission to react to the data with the appropriate emotional response. Is the data good? Then you should feel good. Is the data bad? Then you should feel bad.

So, when you're introducing a slide that shows a sales increase, you could introduce it by saying: "I'm really excited to share this chart with you" or, even better: "I think you'll be excited by this next chart."

Depending on what the data shows, it could be either

disappointing, worrying, alarming or frightening. Or it could be pleasing, fascinating, surprising or amazing.

Allowing yourself to use these adjectives to describe data – even though it may at first seem slightly unusual – will genuinely help to bring a data-based presentation to life for the audience.

Obviously, avoid hyperbole. If the data is exactly as everyone expected it to be, don't pretend it's a phenomenal result. But if there are positives and negatives in the figures, make them live.

Best of both worlds

If your data-based presentation leads to a recommendation (or at least an implied recommendation) or a course of action, apply the basic ideas of *best of both worlds* to it. Present the recommendation both in terms of a positive (what it will lead towards) and in terms of a negative avoided (what it will save the audience from).

If the purpose of your presentation is simply to report, then when you come to your conclusions try to offer both "towards" conclusions and "away from" conclusions – that is, conclusions that lead towards something and conclusions that are about moving away from something. This will create maximum comfort in your audience.

Is the story clear?

When a presenter has a lot of data to convey, it is harder than ever to construct the story from the audience's perspective. It's important therefore, when you've finished writing a presentation or a report, to double check that you have been able to do this. Go over everything and ensure that wherever possible, the story is being told from the perspective of the audience.

A simple tool to help you do this is: *"This is the slide/ paragraph where they ..."*

This involves looking at each slide or paragraph in turn and describing it in terms of what the audience gets out of it. For example:

This is the slide/paragraph where they ... learn about sales in the Midwest.

This is the slide/paragraph where they ... realise that we are spending too much on corporate travel.

This is the slide/paragraph where they ... understand how far we've fallen behind the competition.

If it isn't easy to fill in what words come after those three dots, the first question to ask is: do I need this slide/paragraph at all? If you're sure that you do, ask a colleague to help you try and figure out what comes after the three dots. A fresh pair of eyes can help.

One final thought from Tolstoy (perhaps)

In Chapter 2, when we were defining what a story actually is, we examined many different ideas, but one that we didn't touch on was this:

All great literature is one of two stories. A person goes on a journey or a stranger comes to town.

Like success (and countless quotes you can find on the internet), this idea has many fathers, but it is most commonly attributed to Leo Tolstoy.

In fact, it's likely that no one ever said it *exactly*. Its origins may lie in a writing exercise devised by the novelist John Gardner.[5] Setting his readers the task of writing the opening of a novel, Gardner suggested: "As subject, use either a trip or the arrival of a stranger (some disruption of order – the usual novel beginning)."

Although Gardner doesn't suggest that these two ideas encompass all stories, we can see how closely they relate to Joseph Campbell's monomyth, in which a person does indeed set out on a journey (the hero's journey), which in turn can often be occasioned by the arrival of a stranger.

Why introduce this idea now? Because I have often found in coaching people who have data stories to tell that these two basic plot ideas are helpful analogies for many of the stories that data is required to communicate. Essentially, the analogies work like this:

A person goes on a journey = a company has tried something new. And the presentation is reporting back on data that reveals what happened.

A stranger comes to town = a company has been affected by a sudden and unexpected change in the world or their marketplace. And the presentation is reporting back on data that reveals the effect it had and/or how they reacted.

Given the constant theme of change in most businesses these days – and the relentless arrival of "strangers" in the form of disruptive technology and disrupting competitors – these are two of the most commonly told data stories.

To think of a data story in these storytelling terms – somebody going on a journey or somebody arriving unexpectedly – can help the writer to get beyond the sense of just having a great big wadge of data to communicate and help them to find the story within.

7

The storyteller's mindset

Applying the six-step SUPERB process to documents, emails, case studies and awards entries; using SUPERB as a tool to structure crucial meetings; and how developing a storyteller's mindset can benefit you (and those around you) every day

The last two chapters have shown that you can bring the power of storytelling into work communications by employing three simple tactics:

Always make your audience the hero of the story.

Use storytelling headlines to convey key points.

Structure your work using the SUPERB process.

This approach works effectively for pitches and presentations – after all, standing up and talking to an audience lends itself naturally to storytelling. But in fact, employing (or adapting) these three tactics can enhance any form of communication at work: from a casual chat through to a lengthy document; from an email to a thought-leadership article or blog post.

The same approach can also work well to improve the effectiveness of many types of work meeting, including team-building awaydays, idea-generating sessions and sharing feedback.

The same storytelling methods can apply so effectively across such a broad range of situations because they all depend for their success on strong human-to-human communications. Their effectiveness is improved by our ability to quickly begin to build a relationship with either the recipient of our writing or the other people present in the meeting. This is what these three storytelling tactics do – they help you to build a relationship with your audience. They help you to connect.

This ability to connect is central to what we might call the storyteller's mindset.

When you tell a story about your audience you are making a strong statement: that you care about them, about who they are and about what matters to them. This other-focused, caring attitude lies at the heart of the storyteller's mindset.

Develop a storyteller's mindset

Developing a storyteller's mindset – a focus on the other person, not on yourself – can help you in many areas of work. This doesn't necessarily mean that you will be "telling stories" in all your writing and in all your meetings, although you may do so on occasion. Rather, it means that everything you do will be enhanced by the emotional power that resides in storytelling.

How does a storyteller's mindset come to life at work? It's perhaps easiest to understand if you start with the core storytelling idea that the audience is the hero. Looked at from the other perspective, we could say simply that "it's not about you". Nothing you write and no meeting that you're in should ever have you as the centre of the universe. Ideally, your working day should revolve entirely around others, and you should have no personal agenda.

In a sense, this is of course, completely impossible. You *do* have an agenda. You have a to-do list. There are many things you have to get done. So when you write an email or enter a meeting, you do so with an outcome in mind.

You could argue then that this fundamental idea of having no personal agenda is both disingenuous and unachievable. I can't really argue with this. However, even though it *is* both disingenuous and unachievable, having it as an *aspiration* actually works.

Working as if you don't want anything at all tends to get you everything you want.

Why does this paradoxical idea work? I think the answer lies in one of the most common objections I encounter when training people in this idea: "Isn't this just a slick sales technique?" This objection comes from people who think they are "not in sales" (even though, of course, we are all selling something); and they say the words "sales technique" with a slight curl of the lip to indicate their distaste for the very idea that they might sully their day with such an activity.

What they're asking is: aren't we just *pretending* to care about the other people so as to get our own way? And the answer to this is: if you want it to be just a slick sales technique, it is; but if you choose to genuinely care about the other people that you work with, it isn't. Then it becomes something more.

You can employ these techniques because you're a cunning salesperson. Or you can employ these techniques because you genuinely care about the people around you, and you want to make their day better. Personally, I prefer to take the latter approach – and if you do take the latter approach it comes with many additional benefits in terms of your ongoing relationships both within and outside work. I commend it to you, and I'll continue this chapter on the basis that you genuinely care about the people you work with.

You are, therefore, prepared to put in the extra preparation needed to approach your communications and your meetings with no self-agenda (or with as small a personal agenda as is humanly possible) to reduce your self-orientation, and increase your empathy for those around you. You aspire to find a genuine connection with your colleagues and make them the heroes. You have absorbed the deeper lessons that lie behind the SUPERB process. You have, in short, a storyteller's mindset.

Developing a storyteller's mindset takes practice

This really does take a bit of initial preparation, because our natural location, as we've seen, is within our "tiny skull-sized kingdom", viewing every moment in life as though we are the centre of the universe. We have actively to get ourselves out of this self-oriented perspective and into an other-oriented place.

You can do this by preparing yourself both in general terms for all your work encounters, and then specifically for each individual communication or meeting.

Your general preparation should include making the time to reflect on some of the following points.

Who do I work with who is particularly effective at communicating, making their points clearly and gaining agreement?

How do they do it?

Who around me at work tends to leave people feeling that a meeting with them has gone well?

What is the energy they bring to meetings?

Who around me at work is a particularly good listener?

How do they listen?

What do they do that other people don't do?

What do they not do that other people do?

Who do I often have misunderstandings with?

What could be my *contribution to these misunderstandings?*

How could I communicate with them in a better way?

If you ask yourself these questions and take the time to contemplate the possible answers, you can improve your general communication at work, and take an important shift outside your "tiny skull-sized kingdom".

It's also helpful to have a specific process to prepare before important moments of communications, including meetings, emails and conversations. The idea of preparing or "briefing yourself" for a conversation might seem like overkill, but if you try it, you will be amazed by the difference it makes.

Ask yourself the following questions.

What are my intentions and my desired outcomes? Can I let these go and prioritise instead on the needs of my audience?

How does doing that make me feel?

What would I like people to think, feel or do after this meeting/after reading this document?

How does the thought of having this meeting or writing this document make me feel? Why does it make me feel that way?

How do I think my audience is feeling now?

What are my audience's emotional needs? How do I plan to meet them?

What is the emotional journey I have to guide my audience along? What are the obstacles that I may have to guide them over so that they can complete this journey safely?

The purpose of these questions is to remind yourself of the importance of having a storyteller's mindset: that your priority and focus should not be about getting what you want, but about aligning with the audience, building a relationship with them and meeting their emotional needs.

Fortunately, work creates many opportunities to practise the storyteller's mindset

Adopting a storyteller's mindset won't happen overnight. Learning to focus on others consistently takes time and deliberate practice.

The good news is that work often presents the perfect opportunity to put in the necessary deliberate practice.

Do you ever find yourself in meetings thinking: "What am I even doing here?" Of course you do. It's in the nature of the modern workplace that people find meetings put into their diaries that they really don't need to be in. They have nothing specific to contribute, and nothing much to get out of the meeting, and yet there they are.

These are the meetings where you usually sit thinking: "Well, this is an hour of my life I'm never going to get back." Now you are going to get the hour back. At least, you're going to be able to use the hour as a productive period of deliberate practice which will improve your ability to adopt a storyteller's mindset, helping you develop this beneficial skill.

As you begin the meeting, remind yourself that you genuinely don't have a personal agenda. Until now this would have been a source of frustration for you, but now your task is to accept this fact. Embrace it. You have no personal agenda. You are not the centre of this experience. Go with it!

Do not simply sit there bored and irritated. Instead, actively listen to everybody. Practise doing this so that at the end of the meeting you would be able to write a report that accurately summed up the thoughts, feelings and needs of everyone in the meeting. (You don't actually have to write the report.) Watch people's body language and ask yourself how everyone around you is feeling and why they are feeling that way. Stay open enough that you are sensitive to every mood change in the room.

Don't try to dominate. Don't try to be the smartest person in the room. In fact, don't say anything – but if any opportunity arises where you could offer to help someone, make the offer.

Regularly check in on your own feelings during this meeting. Note how they change as the meeting progresses. At the end of the meeting, take a few moments to reflect on how that meeting felt for you; what it felt like to be there for other people, not for yourself.

If you can practise this regularly, you will more easily be able to take a storyteller's mindset into meetings in which you do have a personal agenda. You will be able to park your agenda, focus on others and their needs – and (paradoxically) achieve your desired outcomes more easily.

Having established how the simple idea that "they are the heroes" can be developed into a more general storyteller's mindset, now let's examine how to use some or all of the stages of the SUPERB process in different forms of communications and meetings.

Emails

Although emails may be short and casual, they still benefit from the application of the SUPERB structure. Because of the brevity of emails, the temptation will be there to skip the *shared experiences* stage, but don't. Alignment is *always* helpful.

If the email is internal – to somebody who you know and have worked with for a while – finding the shared experience should be simple. It can just be a call-back to a comment that they made in a previous meeting, a reminder that they are personally interested in the subject which you are about to bring up. For an email to someone you don't know, finding the shared experience will take more work, but by researching the individual and their company online to find something they have said or something the company believes in you should find the basis of a shared experience.

The *ultimate triumph* should be the way in which you are offering a solution or are going to help the recipient of the email.

You will want to use the *problem definition* stage but in emails you may choose not to use the *explore options and objections* stage, simply to keep the message short. Brevity is, of course, important, but do not omit the *explore objections* stage if you know that the recipient of the email might have objections to your idea. You can't let them go unspoken.

The *real* section is important. Focus on the experience of one person or one team to make what might be a conceptual point as vivid as possible.

Conclude with *best of both worlds*, a positive exciting conclusion but also a reassuring mention of safety.

The table shows what this looks like in practice.

Email text	SUPERB process
Hi Joe, You'll remember that we were discussing how important it is that the company sorts out our hybrid working policy as soon as possible.	*Shared experience*
I think I can make that happen. My team has been exploring various ideas and come up with something that I think could work in the wider company.	*Ultimate triumph*
We talked about how letting everybody do what they want wasn't getting us the results we needed. But that after this long period of working at home, simply imposing a solution would be sub-optimal.	*Problem definition*
My team has come up with a compromise. We developed three possible hybrid solutions, all of which we believed would be effective and then voted on our preferences. So there was an element of control but also an element of choice. We ended up with a solution that seems to work for us and I think it might be the way to go company-wide.	*Explore options*
If you like, I could put together a workstream to identify the three most popular hybrid solutions that would achieve the minimum days in the office that you require, and hook up with the employee resource groups to discuss how a vote could be handled.	*Real*
Potentially this could get people back collaborating in person in the way you want without causing too much resistance or too many issues for the People Team.	*Best of both worlds*

Documents

To illustrate how the SUPERB structure works with documents, let's take the example of a white paper or discussion document about diversity designed for circulation within a company. (Essentially the same structure would work for a thought-leadership article on the same subject designed for wider circulation outside the company, although the content would naturally be different.)

It's tempting to try to begin with an impactful, confrontational, controversial or exciting opening to grab the reader's attention. Resist this temptation. Instead begin with a shared experience to gain their alignment and agreement.

Here's how the document might start:

Document text	SUPERB process
After much discussion over the past couple of years, we are all aware that diversity is one of those rare subjects which offers us a chance to do something that is good for the company, good for us all as individuals and good for a wider society.	*Shared experiences*
This paper outlines a new approach that should help us to tackle the very real challenges that we have faced in this area, to achieve the diverse workforce we aspire to and to establish a genuinely inclusive culture.	*Ultimate triumph*
However, we are also all aware that meeting our diversity targets has proved to be a slower and more difficult process, particularly at senior levels, than we had hoped.	*Problem definition*

From here on the body of the document will concern itself with more detailed *problem definition* and will *explore options and objections*.

It is standard practice to list all the challenges first and then put together one overall solution. However, to maintain a storytelling structure, it is much better to tackle one problem at a time, explore the options, pose your preferred solution, deal with any objections and then move on to the next problem.

This gives us the up-and-down, conflict/resolution shape of a story. In this case, the structure might look like this:

State the problems the company has faced identifying finding diverse talent

Explore options

State preferred solution

Discuss potential objections

Propose workarounds

State the problems the company has faced recruiting diverse talent

Explore options

State preferred solution

Discuss potential objections

Propose workarounds

State the problems the company has faced onboarding diverse talent

Explore options

State preferred solution

Discuss potential objections

Propose workarounds

and so on.

That may seem a bit formulaic and repetitive, but in practice it won't be. If you write the document following this structure, it will be easy to read, easy to follow and memorable, because it will be following the storytelling structure that engages readers.

The *real* stage should be used to give one or two case studies of individual experiences – ideally individual experiences that show a positive vision of the future. You can then continue the *real* section by adding a proposed timeline or suggested series of next steps to meet the readers' emotional need for support.

Finally, add a *best of both worlds* conclusion which offers both a positive vision of the future and a reassuring guarantee.

Using storytelling headlines as subheadings throughout the document helps the reader to progress easily through the text and acts as a helpful "executive summary" to those who skim.

Case studies

Case studies can follow the SUPERB process precisely.

Use *shared experiences* to set up the context of the industry or sector by making a statement that everyone will agree with.

Use the *ultimate triumph* section to outline the results you achieved early in the case study.

Use *problem definition* and *explore options and objections* to provide the structure of the body of the case study, recounting what happened in terms of conflict/resolution.

Make it *real* by giving one specific, vivid example of how the work you are discussing showed up in the lives of a customer, colleague or other stakeholder (as appropriate). Use *best of both worlds* to explain the detailed results in terms of both positive forward-looking achievements and in terms of how you avoided any potential downsides.

Awards entries

Awards entries follow the same basic structure as case studies. However, there is another layer of *ultimate triumph* that can be applied to all awards entries.

The audience for an awards entry comprises the judges. These are usually individuals who have reached a certain status within the industry, which means they have come on the radar of awards organisers, who have reached out and asked them to give up their time unpaid to judge the awards. Flattered and seeking to give back something to the industry, they have agreed. Then, months later, the actual work hits them. They have no time to do this work, but they are committed. So, they now need to undergo a "triage" process finding as quickly as possible those few awards entries that are worth further discussion and discarding the majority.

The *ultimate triumph* for the judges is that you help them to decide quickly whether your entry goes on the "possible" or the "discards" pile. You can help them to achieve this by writing a three-sentence summary at the beginning of the awards entry.

Even if there isn't a section headed "Summary", begin whatever the opening section is with your summary. You may be bending the format slightly, but that's fine because you're making the judges' lives easier.

Your summary has one sentence stating what the most difficult challenge was, a second sentence stating what the most brilliant thing you did was and a third sentence stating what the best results you achieved were. No more.

These three sentences allow the judges to decide instantly whether your entry is a contender. And, in fact, by caring enough about the judges to understand and meet their most pressing need you have instantly increased your chances of winning an award.

Storytelling structure makes meetings better too

Is it too much of a stretch to suggest that the storytelling structure can help us not only to write better presentations and documents but also to hold better meetings? Not at all.

One of the primary roles of a story is to form an emotional bond between the teller of the story and the audience. A similar emotional bond should be the objective you bring into any meeting: not getting what you want, but building a relationship or continuing to build a relationship with the other people in the meeting.

And just as a story has a clear narrative structure, a well-managed meeting also has a narrative structure. People in the meeting should feel that they are on a journey and that they are getting somewhere.

Let's look at a few typical meetings that you might have at work and examine how the fundamentals of storytelling and the *SUPERB* process can enhance them.

Team-building awayday

An awayday designed to help a cross-functional team to bond at the beginning of a project can be a source of dread both for those charged with structuring it and with some of those who have to go on it and who are no great fans of icebreakers, sharing truths about themselves or being forced into organised fun activities ("funishment", as one client of mine refers to them).

Structuring a team-building awayday around the SUPERB process will make it easier to create, less daunting to attend and more effective in reaching its aim.

Instead of a wacky game to break the ice, or those horrific "share something with the group that we don't know about you" moments, it's far better to begin the day in a place of agreement and alignment. So, devise an opening exercise that allows the team members – strangers as they might be – to find common ground and *shared experiences*.

One of the best ways of doing this is to split the team into groups, and have each group discuss what they think makes a great team and what they think makes a terrible team (with examples allowed from previous employment, but not from their time with the current company).

The groups share their thoughts with the wider team, with everything captured on Post-its. You can build a "wall of fame" and a "wall of shame" showing respectively what the team believes makes for a good team, and for a bad team. You will inevitably find a broad level of agreement on what makes a great team and what makes a terrible team, so the "wall of fame" and "wall of shame" create deep *shared experiences* as well as then serving as an aspiration and a warning sign respectively as the day progresses.

After this opening exercise, revealing the *ultimate triumph* is simple. It's the fact that you are aiming to emulate the teams on your "wall of fame" and avoid the pitfalls made all too clear on the "wall of shame".

Structuring the body of the day around *problem definition* and then *explore options and objections* makes perfect sense:

What are the tasks that the team must accomplish?

What are the different ways in which they could accomplish them and which ones do we prefer?

Given our preferred choices, what obstacles might they meet, and how will they work around them?

It's all too easy for such exercises to stay in the realm of the abstract. Adding a *real* stage in which you work through one specific example of an actual task and how it would involve actual people, actual tools and processes and meetings and reports will stress-test your ideas to make sure they are relevant and actionable.

Your opening exercise gives you a perfect *best of both worlds* end to the day. Look at the work you've done. See how you aligned with the "wall of fame" and avoided the "wall of shame".

Idea-generation session

Again, instead of having a wacky exercise to break the ice and make people more creative (for some reason, that doesn't seem to work), begin in a place of agreement by setting everyone some easy pre-homework. Ask them to identify some great creativity that they've come across in any medium at all (work-related or otherwise) that they are going to share with the group in a quick three-minute show and tell.

Not everybody will agree with everything but you will find a broad consensus on many of the points about what great ideas look like, creating a sense of *shared experiences*.

Make clear the aim of the day – your collective *ultimate triumph* – where you want to end up and also where you don't want to end up. Be very specific. If you're expecting to have finished ideas at the end of the day, say so. But if more realistically you are expecting to have done a lot of development work which will need finishing off another time, make that clear so that everybody knows not just what direction you're heading in, but how far you expect to get.

Then, *problem definition*: clarify the exact challenges which you are generating ideas to overcome. And *explore options and objections*: task groups or individuals not with coming up with an idea but with coming up with several options, exploring how each would work and looking at what could possibly go wrong with them and what can be done about it.

If you have enough people, divide into three groups, and rotate the work.

Phase	Group 1	Group 2	Group 3
1	Generate ideas A1, A2 and A3	Generate ideas B1, B2 and B3	Generate ideas C1, C2 and C3
2	Show how ideas C1, C2 and C3 can be executed	Show how ideas A1, A2 and A3 can be executed	Show how ideas B1, B2 and B3 can be executed
3	Look at how ideas B1, B2 and B3 could go wrong and develop workarounds	Look at how ideas C1, C2 and C3 could go wrong and develop workarounds	Look at how ideas A1, A2 and A3 could go wrong and develop workarounds

For the *real* section, ask groups to explore how the ideas would impact the days of either a typical customer, supplier or an internal department. How practical are these ideas?

Finally in the wider group, look at the ideas you've ended up with, and rank them using a *best of both worlds* approach, looking for ideas that combine innovative, exciting creativity with the ability to work in the real world.

Giving feedback

Giving feedback can be a sensitive and tricky task, given the egos involved and the fact that the very existence of a feedback meeting often implies that something isn't working as well it could. In a work environment where management behaviour and language that would have been standard practice in some environments a decade ago are now seen as bullying, the task has become even harder. How can you communicate potentially difficult and uncomfortable truths without upsetting or offending?

The SUPERB model is a very helpful structure for feedback sessions. It can minimise damage to egos and improve learnings for the future. So, if you have to give someone feedback, how should you do it?

As ever, the alignment of the *shared experiences* stage is vital. Remember the ideas of relationship expert John Gottman that we discussed in Chapter 5: a meeting that begins in agreement is more likely to end in agreement. You really need a session like this to end in agreement; otherwise it is simply a waste of everyone's time, potentially damaging the relationship between you and the receiver of feedback, while not improving the latter's performance or behaviour.

A natural way to start in agreement is by reviewing the overall objectives of the team and the overall targets of the individual. (If this is not a place of agreement, then you have a bigger problem.)

The *ultimate triumph* of this session is *not* the successful transmission of the feedback or the telling off of an individual. Remember, the hero of this meeting is not you. The hero is the person to whom you are giving the feedback. The *ultimate triumph* that we are seeking is that the individual gets better at their job and learns something. Additionally, the team they work in will get better as a result. This needs to be clear before the feedback is given.

The *problem definition* stage is where the feedback is introduced. Be very clear and specific about the performance issue or behaviour that has been observed and that needs to change.

Then instead of telling the person what you think needs to happen, *explore options* with them. What are the different ways in which this could be tackled? You can still state your preferred solution, but by first exploring options you have allowed the individual concerned to state their preferences and their objections. You are also, therefore, putting forward your proposed next steps not as a perfect solution, but as a recommended way of improving the situation.

Then make it as *real* as possible. You may know exactly what you mean when you say you want someone to be more conscientious or a better team-player, but why should anyone else? What would the new behaviour look like? Give some day-to-day examples. How would they be different in a meeting? How would they write emails differently? How would they address colleagues differently? Spell it out. Emphasise the *best of both worlds* nature of adopting the feedback, that it will be a win-win situation, better for everybody involved.

*

You can see even from the examples in this chapter that developing a storyteller's mindset and employing the SUPERB storytelling process can help with many types of writing and enhance many occasions at work. Take the time to consider how you could apply them to the work situations that you face regularly, especially those that you sometimes struggle with, or where you feel there may be potential to improve your performance and your outcomes.

If you're not sure exactly how to start to apply them, it always helps to begin with the fundamental perspective shift: "It's not about me." Reassess each situation by wondering, if you're no longer the centre of the universe, how does this change things? How will you behave and communicate differently? You'll be surprised at the difference this simple shift can make.

8

The emotional journey

**Understanding the eight key emotional triggers that
underpin the storytelling model; taking your audience
on an emotional journey towards agreement; and why
storytelling is even better when it's collaborative**

A bearded, bedraggled man walks through a half-ruined and
yet still majestic building. He is heavily manacled and led
by a guard. The man is here for sentencing, and his guard's
contemptuous expression suggests that the sentence will be
severe.

Together, they approach a group of seated figures. The
bearded man's appearance speaks of a long stay in jail. The
appearance of the group that he is approaching speaks of
privilege and power. A canopy shades them from the hot sun.

Surprisingly, and much to the guard's disgust, it is the
bearded man who somehow takes control of proceedings. He
starts to give an impassioned speech.

Spoiler Alert. If you haven't seen the final episode of *Game of
Thrones*, but are planning to do so one day, you may not want to
read the next few paragraphs.

The man, Tyrion Lannister, begins to speak about unity.

"What unites people?" he asks. "Armies? Gold? Flags?" None of the other characters answer. But, given everything we know about them and the recent history of the lands they govern, we can guess that their answer to the question would be: "None of the above."

So what does unite people? Tyrion answers his own question. "Stories!" he says. "There's nothing in the world more powerful than a good story. Nothing can stop it. No enemy can defeat it."

So passionately does Tyrion believe in stories that he argues that the new ruler of the Seven Kingdoms should not be the person with the mightiest army, or the person possessed of the finest diplomatic skills, but the person with the best story. "Who has a better story than Bran the Broken, the boy who fell from High Tower and lived. He knew he'd never walk again. So he learned to fly. He is the keeper of all our stories. Who better to lead us into the future?"

In *Game of Thrones* then, after eight seasons of intrigue, deception, war and destruction, the best story wins.

Tyrion knows – and, having reached this stage of this book, you know too – that the power of storytelling lies in its ability to make an emotional connection. Stories bring people together. Stories unify.

Just as we can see storytelling in terms of a structure – a narrative flow – we can also see it in terms of the emotional journey that the storyteller takes their audience on, and in the way that a storyteller connects with their audience and then stays connected.

As a storyteller you must take your audience on an emotional journey and, in most instances, the end point of this journey is a place of agreement. There will be a desired outcome: an obvious (or implied) decision that you want someone to make, or some behavioural change that you want to happen. You want your audience to do, think or feel something that they might not have done, thought or felt before; to start a new behaviour, to stop a certain behaviour or at least to modify their behaviour in some way.

Diplomacy has been defined as the art of building bridges for people to climb down gracefully. Similarly, you might define workplace storytelling as the art of building a road *along which people are prepared to travel* that gets them to the place you want them to be. Remember that decisions are made for emotional reasons, not logical reasons; you must always keep in mind that this journey you are asking them to embark upon is an emotional one.

This chapter looks more closely at the emotional effect that these stages are designed to have. Then, as you become more skilled in using the storytelling structure, you will also be able to improvise around it, bringing in other elements that have the same emotional effect at the right stage of the communication.

We are going to focus on eight basic human emotional needs drawn from various scientific areas of study that are concerned with human motivation: evolutionary psychology, self-determination theory, attachment theory, transactional analysis and neuro-linguistic programming.

They don't, though, require a deep-dive into any of these disciplines or theories. All that matters here is that these specific ideas work – and they do.

They are the emotional needs that most commonly have to be met for an audience to conclude:

"That meeting went well."

"I agree with what I've just heard."

"That is definitely an idea is worth pursuing."

"I want to work with that person."

Looked at another way, they are the eight emotional needs which, if they are not met, will cause a communication to end badly, or at least in a place of non-agreement.

The eight needs are:

1. the need for alignment
2. the need for emotional connection
3. the need for structure
4. the need for recognition
5. the need for ownership
6. the need for stimulus
7. the need for safety
8. the need for support.

As in previous chapters, I will spend what might at first glance appear to be a disproportionate amount of time discussing the need for alignment. This is because without alignment, none of the rest will work; and also because it is the need that is most often overlooked.

The need for alignment

Start where they are

It's important in any communication to "start where they are". This is usually taken to mean that you should begin a piece of communication at a place which reflects the level of knowledge the audience has about the subject at hand.

This is certainly one aspect of "start where they are". However, it's also important to "start where they are" in terms of their specific *relationship* to a topic. So, if you are giving a presentation about climate change to a group of activists, you do not have to begin by showing them the data that proves the existence of climate change. They already know that. And if you are presenting to the chief finance officer about your company's sustainability strategy, they will want to know as much about the costs and financial benefits as they will about the rights and wrongs of sustainable behaviour.

But you can take "start where they are" much further than this. You can truly "start where they are" *emotionally.*

There is a saying which is often attributed to the first-century philosopher Philo of Alexandria:

> Be kind, because everyone you meet is fighting a battle you cannot see.

This saying is undoubtedly true. In fact, I would suggest it doesn't go far enough. My suggestion is that we rewrite it as:

> Be kind, because everyone you meet is fighting *many* battles you cannot see.

This basic conflict/resolution, challenge/solution dynamic of storytelling has arisen largely because it reflects how we tend to see our lives. Each of our lives can be seen as a series of *parallel* stories of where we want to be, what is stopping us getting there and what we are attempting to do to overcome those challenges.

This basic storytelling shape exists, for example, in your everyday "to do" lists. How often do you get everything on your "to do" list finished? If you're like most people, the answer is almost never; your day takes the form of a story, which comprises your quest to get these things done, the series of challenges you encounter that make this quest harder and harder, and your valiant attempts to overcome those challenges.

This is just *one* of your stories. You are likely to have several other ongoing stories where your life is not currently how you want it to be, and where you have therefore embarked on a quest to attain a certain goal or to restore balance to your life. Each story encompasses one or more battles.

These battles may include, but are certainly not limited to, the following.

The money battle. I'm only guessing here, but maybe you don't have enough money. You're either struggling to pay the bills at the end of the month or struggling to find the money for a deposit on a flat or struggling to find the money for the mortgage, or childcare, or the care of elderly parents or your own retirement. There is almost always a money battle.

The family of origin battle. Each person's family battle will be unique but many of them will share similar qualities. You may have an ongoing battle with your parents many years after you've left home. There is a way you want them to see you and it is not the way that they do see you. You may have an ongoing battle with siblings who still treat you the way they treated you when you were schoolkids.

The family battle. You may have an ongoing battle with your children. There is a way you want them to behave and it's not the way they actually behave. There is a world view that you are trying to impart to them, and they're not remotely interested in it. There may be a series of small-scale battles with your partner, or your whole relationship may feel like a war of attrition.

The time battle. There is probably something you would really like to do (or do more of), which you never have time to do.

In fact, there are probably several things that you would really like to do that you never have time to do. But there may be one overarching ambition that is continually put off because the time just isn't there.

The work battle. Of course, there is never just *one* work battle. There are several work battles going on at any one time. You may have several customer battles going on. You may have several battles going on with internal stakeholders. You may have a battle going on with your boss. You may have a battle going on with your team. All these relationships are constantly *not quite the way you want them to be*, and you are battling to get them to your desired state. The battles can seem endless.

On top of all of these, some people will be fighting health battles and mental health battles, which may be occupying a huge amount of their time, resources and psychological capital. They may also be in battles with noisy neighbours, with the council, with the tax authorities.

When you communicate with anyone at work, to *truly* "start where they are" you have to understand how all these battles are currently shaping their emotional state, what preoccupies them and what really matters to them.

You are not the most important thing in their day. You are not the thing they care most about. You are not the centre of their universe. To truly "start where they are" requires a full acknowledgement and acceptance of this fact. And your understanding of this fact has to radiate out from every aspect of your communications.

If you act or talk as though you are the most important person in the room or the absolute centre of their attention right now, you have already set up a significant barrier to the success of your communication.

The storyteller's question

Can we go even deeper? Can we do an even better job of starting where they are than by simply acknowledging our relative unimportance? Yes, we can. We can choose to find out more about their battles.

You can choose to show that you care more about them than about your own agenda.

The self-improvement pioneer Dale Carnegie once wrote: "You can make more friends in two months by becoming interested in other people, than you can in two years by trying to get people interested in you." Equally you can make more progress in a meeting by spending five minutes being interested in the other person than by spending an hour talking about yourself.

You need to learn to suspend your ego, putting the other individual's wants and needs ahead of your own. You need to listen and to engage in a conversation in a way that is not simply waiting until the other person stops talking so that you can say what you were going to say anyway.

You need to step outside your "tiny skull-sized kingdom".

Before you *tell* them a story, you need to *ask* them about *their* stories, because a storyteller is as interested in hearing stories as they are in telling them.

So how do you remove yourself from the centre of the universe? One of the most powerful techniques for doing this emerged not from my experience in business but from my parallel career as a music journalist.

From time to time, on press trips, a group of us music journalists would find ourselves together in a hotel lobby, a cafe or a bar. We would compare notes on the musician we had interviewed or were preparing to interview, or others who we had spent time with. If we had a lot of time, the talk would turn more generally to the theory of interviewing: how to optimise the usually limited amount of time we had to spend with our interview subjects and how best, in that brief period of time, to break through the carefully constructed barriers that most musicians and other artists and celebrities have been trained to construct.

A theory emerged that there might be a perfect opening question – the holy grail of questions – and if you could begin the interview with this one question, the rest of the interview would flow perfectly. Over time, the idea evolved that if you got the first question right you wouldn't even need any further questions. There was in effect one question to unlock them all. Ask this question and answer after answer would cascade from the interview subject, with the merest prompt (an occasional "Oh really?" or perhaps "Tell me more").

I can't say for certain how seriously *all* the other journalists took this idea, but I know that a couple of others, like myself, took it very seriously indeed. We proceeded to test the effectiveness of initial questions, monitoring exactly how they affected the rest of the interview. In the end, we came up with the one question which, it turns out, does unlock everything:

How is your day going?

It doesn't sound much, does it? In fact it's remarkably simple, natural and conversational. However, having said that, sticking to the exact wording is vital.

The following variations *don't* work:

How are you doing?

How's it going?

How are you?

How is everything?

What's up?

It has to be "How is your day going?"

I found that any interview that began with that question flowed better, went deeper, and led to more openness from the interview subject. We moved beyond the superficial agenda to engage in a genuine conversation about their life and the challenges they were facing.

Taking this idea and transferring it into work communications, I found that it worked equally well as a device to create alignment at the beginning of meetings, one-to-ones or even casual conversations.

The key learning here is that if you ask first about *their* stories, then *your* story gains more power.

Crucially, you have to ask "How is your day going?" not as a casual greeting, but as a genuine request for information from someone who actually cares about how their day is going. Having this attitude – the storyteller's mindset – is as vital as getting the wording right.

If you ask it as a casual greeting, you will get the answer "Fine". But if you ask it as a genuine request for information, you will get an answer that hints at one of the battles outlined above. The hint might come in the words they say, or it might be there in a roll of the eyes, a sigh or a shrug.

At this point one more slight prompt is needed.

What's that look about?

That was a big sigh!

Tell me more ...

And then ... allow the silence.

Don't say anything.

And within a few seconds they will be talking you through one of their key battles.

Lose control

Admittedly there are several objections you might have to beginning a work meeting, for example, in this way.

1. There isn't any time for idle chat.
2. There are too many people in the room.
3. I'll lose control of the meeting.

It's certainly true that there is limited time in most work meetings, and we could always do with a bit more. However, time spent meeting the *need for alignment* is never wasted.

Also, most meetings involve a period when people are settling down, finding a seat, making coffee, setting up the tech, ringing someone from IT to *help* set up the tech, finishing an email, leaving a quick voicemail message.

While everybody else treats it like dead time, this is your opportunity to use it to ask the simple "How is your day going?" question.

It doesn't matter that there are others in the room. You're talking to one individual. You may choose to speak to the most important person in the room, or you may choose to speak to the person sitting next to you. You're simply engaging one of your audience in a conversation that *isn't* about you and *is* about them.

Also, people share many of their battles, in broad terms, if not in detail. Once this conversation starts you are likely to find that others join it.

The third objection – "I'll lose control of the meeting" – is the one that tends to worry people most.

But you *want* to lose control of the meeting. This is exactly what moving outside your "tiny skull-sized kingdom" means: giving up control.

It isn't a problem at all to go where the audience wants to go. You might lose control of your carefully structured agenda. You might lose control of exactly how much time you have to make each point on each slide. But you have *not* lost control of the emotional journey that you want to take the other person on. Quite the opposite. You have begun that emotional journey extremely powerfully.

Even when there are a few people out there – the "Can we just cut to the chase?" people – who will bat away the "How is your day going?" question with a "Yeah, fine", don't worry. Although they are not willing to share their battle, they have registered the question and the tone in which you ask it and in their own reserved way they have allowed a measure of alignment.

Once you're aligned, stay aligned

It's vital to create alignment at the beginning, but alignment remains helpful at all stages of any communication. You want the audience to regularly notice that they are broadly in agreement with you on a number of topics. The more things they agree with you on, the more likely they are to agree with your final point or recommendation. If possible, use more *shared experiences* regularly throughout written communications, or check in with your audience regularly during verbal communications with enrolling questions to ensure that alignment is maintained.

It can be very easy to forget to do this. So, find a way to fix it firmly in your storytelling structure. For example, one way to do this is to make *shared experiences* or enrolling questions a regular part of your navigation throughout a presentation. You could use the enrolling questions technique whenever there is a transition from one point on an agenda to the next point.

"We've all had a chance to introduce ourselves, haven't we?"

"We've seen – haven't we? – that there is plenty of evidence for our assertion that automation will be a priority for the business in the coming year."

"The sales data shows – doesn't it? – that the arrival of this new competitor has seriously disrupted the market."

As you become more confident in the use of this technique, or when you find yourself in situations where you are reasonably confident of the mood and mindset of your audience, you can move beyond enrolling questions to questions that require an answer and then pause to elucidate the "Yes" from your audience.

"Am I right in thinking that you know everyone on the team today?"

"Are you happy that we've covered this area in enough detail? And are you ready to move on?"

Enrolling questions do not have to be answered verbally or even elicit a physical nod; there is an internal agreement happening which is the emotional effect you're trying to get. However, if you can elicit a nod or a verbal "Yes", that is an even stronger level of alignment.

Pre-planning to use these questions at transitional points in your communications will help to ensure that you do not skip over this vital technique but rather have regular moments of conscious alignment and agreement from your audience throughout.

An audience who agrees with you again and again will find it hard to disagree with your final recommendation. You have become someone that they agree with, someone whose thinking mirrors theirs and someone whose opinions they seem to share.

The need for emotional connection

Storytelling structure gives you an emotional connection with your audience that a traditional benefit-led, bullet-pointed communication can never hope to achieve. Using storytelling headlines anchors you in storytelling language, reducing the friction of psychological reactance that simply stating an argument would create.

You can deepen the emotional connection by maintaining the use of storytelling language throughout everything you say. For example, always stick to plain English and avoid all business jargon and acronyms.

It's tempting to use your company's favourite jargon because everyone is familiar with it, and it can be even more tempting to use a customer's jargon and acronyms because it seems to be a way of suggesting closeness.

Unfortunately, even jargon that everyone knows can sabotage your attempts at storytelling. Try to remove as much jargon as possible or bring it as close to everyday language as you can manage, for example:

"in the second half of the year" is preferable to "in Q3 and Q4"

"achieve all our targets" is preferable to "100% completion of KPIs"

"talk about this later" is preferable to "take this offline"

You can further emphasise the storytelling nature of your

presentation by using two-part sentences that employ the problem/resolution, challenge/solution structure of stories. You don't want to overdo these, but used carefully at important moments in your presentation, they heighten the emotional effect of everything around them.

"Nothing we've talked about so far will have any effect at all ... unless we get the execution right."

"There is a huge amount of fake news, lies and misinformation out there on this subject ... but there is also one perennial truth that we can hang on to."

"Some companies search in vain for years to find the solution to this problem ... but the answer lies within your own company and we can help you reveal it."

"We've been down this path before and it's a path that has led us astray ... but this time is going to be different."

This two-part structure, which builds up tension and uncertainty and then immediately resolves it is a classic storytelling tactic. Return to this device at key turning points, and you will clearly establish your role as a storyteller, which will in turn maintain your emotional connection with the audience.

The need for structure

You will make your audience more comfortable if you have a clear agenda and structure to your communications.

As we've already seen in this chapter, the audience members are allowed to take a meeting away from your agenda and leave any structure behind. That is their prerogative and you should be prepared, within reason, to follow them wherever they want to go. But you need to have brought with you the reassurance and comfort of a structure, which can always be returned to.

For example, you can give a clear agenda and structure within PowerPoint. Agenda slides can be made clear and visually distinct from the other slides, built to show the whole agenda, then highlight the point you've just made and then highlight the point you're moving on to. This emphasises the story and its causal flow, rather than merely signposting the next point. It gives clear signalling to anyone in the audience whose focus might have drifted off, giving them every opportunity to get back on board and continue the journey.

Slides can be colour coded so that either different sections are coloured differently or different types of slides are coloured distinctly to help an audience understand where they are in the story. One of the biggest mistakes people make with PowerPoint is to have all the slides in the presentation adhering to a strict template. A degree of consistency is, of course, a good thing, but a strict sameness throughout the presentation can be confusing.

Use progress bars on slides that move along in the same way as you might see along the bottom of a YouTube video. That gives a clear indication of how far you are into the presentation. And how much is left.

You can also provide a printed agenda and (if you're presenting to another company) biographies of your team so that the audience does not have to wait to establish where they are. They can clarify for themselves what's going on at any time.

It also creates a helpful structure for shy or introverted people to talk to others and ask questions without encountering the social awkwardness of having forgotten people's names or not being quite sure who to talk to about what.

The need for recognition and the need for ownership

We'll look at these two human needs together as the techniques employed to make sure that they are met are similar and complementary. The *need for recognition* is connected to the idea that frames the whole story: that the audience is the hero of the story, not you.

As well as making the story about the audience, you also want them to contribute to the story, so that they feel even more deeply that it's their story. This brings you into the area of discovery where they work with you to co-create, rather than sitting back passively and listening to your ideas.

The strength of this is confirmed by research carried out by Kimberly Elsbach of the University of California, Davis and Roderick Kramer of Stanford University.[1] Elsbach and Kramer studied Hollywood pitch meetings across a six-year period. The most important finding of the research was that the success of a pitch depends largely on the contribution of "the catcher" (the studio executives who were the audiences for the pitches). Many writers think that the studio executives they are pitching to are just "suits" whose ideas should be disregarded. However, writers who involved the catcher in the creative process, allowing them to contribute creatively, were significantly more successful in selling their ideas.

"Once the catcher feels like a creative collaborator, the odds of rejection diminish," according to Elsbach, who offers the advice: "Find a part of your proposal that you're willing to yield on and invite the catcher to come up with suggestions."

Commenting on this research in his book *To Sell Is Human*, Daniel Pink says: "The purpose of a pitch isn't necessarily to move others immediately to adopt your idea. The purpose is to offer something so compelling that it begins a conversation, brings the other person in as a participant, and eventually arrives at an outcome that appeals to both of you."

One obstacle that we might encounter here is that the "catcher", your audience, may feel that their role is to sit back and listen. How then do we engage them in collaboration? The simplest way to do this is to identify part of your proposal on which you are willing to allow some wiggle room and then introduce it not as a fully formed idea, but as an option which you are possibly slightly reluctant to bring forward.

A construction like "I'm not entirely sure that this is appropriate for you, but I'd be interested to know what you think of it ..." should be enough to bring out helpful feedback from the audience. The slight suggestion that maybe you weren't even going to bring this idea to their attention seems to add an intriguing quasi-scarcity effect. Instead of hearing "This possibly isn't for you", the audience seems to hear "This might be very interesting indeed."

You've opened a gate through which your audience can take on the role of collaborator and even if they come back with "I don't think it's quite right for us as it is," the process of discovery has begun. Your audience has been given both *recognition* (you have implied that their expertise is more relevant here than your opinion) and *ownership* (they have become involved in the creation of your story).

Some people worry that giving your audience recognition and ownership implicitly reduces your own status. In fact, inviting others to contribute and even suggesting that their view might be more important than yours seems to *add* to the esteem in which you are held by the audience.

Jonah Berger, a marketing professor at the Wharton School at the University of Pennsylvania, explains this phenomenon.

Asking for advice doesn't actually make us look worse, it actually makes us look better. Asking for advice makes us look smarter and more competent because people are egocentric. We inherently love giving advice, we think we give good advice, we think we're smart and have good thoughts. So when someone else comes up to us and asks us for our advice, we think, "Wow, they must be pretty smart because of all the people they could have asked, they asked me."

The need for stimulus

We all know that sitting in a meeting, watching a presentation or reading a lengthy document for any extended period of time can be boring. Even if the subject is one that we know we should be paying attention to, even if the presenter or writer is perfectly competent, our attention wanders.

Human beings need stimulus – more stimulus than the average work meeting or document provides. If you provide stimulus, you will find it easier to maintain people's interest.

For example, in a pitch, you can provide additional stimulus in the way you present and through the use of objects in the room.

In PowerPoint, a presenter has maybe five seconds of guaranteed attention when they put a new slide up. Simply by using more slides to build your message point by point, you can actively use each build as the moment to introduce a significant piece of information that takes the story forward.

There is a received wisdom in many businesses that slides "take a minute" – and that you can judge the length of time a presentation will take by counting the number of slides. First, this is nonsense. Second, it tends to make people think that they are *supposed* to go through their presentation devoting the same amount of time to each slide. How boring!

You can add stimulus simply by varying the amount of time you devote to slides. If you feel you need to devote a long period of time to one slide, follow it with five slides that you click through in 10 seconds each.

This is another reason to avoid templates that are overly consistent. If a new subject matter brings with it a fresh colour or a fresh shape or a fresh design, this naturally adds stimulus.

Think about the way that you interact with the slides. Again, avoid sameness. Sometimes you might be standing next to the slides. Sometimes you might be sitting in front of them. Sometimes you might be walking to the back of the room to become part of the audience as you all look at the slides together. You may *sometimes* even do the thing that we're all taught not to do; turn your back and read a slide. If there is one really critical piece of information, it does no harm at all to turn your attention to the slide and read it word for word slowly and carefully. The change in your behaviour provides the stimulus, as does turning back to face the audience afterwards to deliver a particularly exciting point.

Virtual meetings require you to give even more thought to how you are going to relate with your slides and ask your audience to relate to them, since you are not in control of how each individual has their screen set up, and it's harder to pick up on body language changes as individuals start to become restless. A useful approach is to imagine that instead of being in another location staring at a different screen, you are sitting next to them and looking at the same laptop. In this situation a presenter naturally becomes more overtly directional ("See that red bar there," "If you scan to the bottom of the slide, you'll see …"). This approach works better in virtual meetings than simply changing slides and carrying on with a script, without actively referencing the new slide.

The need for safety

You primarily meet the *need for safety* by finishing your communications using the *best of both worlds* step from the SUPERB process, ensuring you are speaking the language both of "towards" people and "away from" people.

Always remember that there is a tendency to use more "towards" language than "away from" language because there is a common belief that you want to be forward-looking, that you want to talk about innovation and reinvention, that the new is automatically exciting, and that it brings benefits that everyone will naturally be keen on. This isn't true. Make sure you insert some "away from" language throughout.

This can be extremely clear: include phrases like "Don't worry" and "Let me reassure you", and words like "safe", "reliable" and "guaranteed". If you think those words sound a bit boring, you are probably a "towards" person, and so you *really* need to make sure you add some of that language. Make sure you find room for words that promise security as well as for the words that promise excitement.

The need for support

When you're communicating ideas, it's easy to get carried away with the cleverness of them. Remember that ideas are not what really matters. When it comes down to it, what makes a difference is the execution. A good enough idea that a business can make happen is infinitely preferable to a brilliant idea that it can't.

In any story that involves new ideas, new processes, new tools, new systems or new ways of working, you must take the time to show how the new thing will be implemented and how you will support your audience in this period.

You need to answer the audience's potential questions (*before* they have to ask them):

What happens next?

What do I have to do?

What does my team have to do?

How will you help me and how will you help them?

In other words, your story doesn't stop when your story stops.

To the extent that it is possible, you want to walk your audience through the process. Show them the dashboard on their laptop and let them click on it, or tell them exactly how many meetings will have to go in their diary, at what intervals and with whom.

People will be resistant to change even if you show them a wonderful vision of the future unless you also give them simple, actionable first steps. And quick wins. It's not enough to say that things will get better – they have to get tangibly better quickly. If the people that you are selling to are going to have to sell your idea to their bosses, they need to believe that, reasonably soon, they will be able to point to an improvement and effectively say to their bosses, "See – I was right."

If you meet this emotional need, as with all the needs outlined in this chapter, you increase the power of your storytelling and the success of your communications. Understanding the needs that storytelling can meet, and knowing that every communication is about taking your audience on an emotional journey – one that leads to a place of agreement – may not lead to you governing the Seven Kingdoms (although I wouldn't rule it out), but it will give you a significant competitive advantage at work.

9

The writing process

Confronting the blank sheet of paper; understanding writers' "trade secrets" that make the writing process easier; knowing above all that writing is rewriting; and getting some very good advice from George Orwell and Stephen King

It's a cold December's night in London in 1931, a week before Christmas, but there's little Christmas cheer in evidence as a young man is led up the steps to Bethnal Green police station.

The man, who gives his name as Edward Burton, is charged with being drunk and incapable. His story is simple and sad: having been sacked from his job in a draper's shop and disowned by his family because of habitual drunkenness, he is scraping a living by taking casual work as a porter at Billingsgate Fish Market. He admits to having drunk several pints of beer and most of a bottle of whiskey that evening before making a scene in a local public house.

Burton spends the night in a holding cell before being taken to Old Street Police Court where, on the advice of the duty constable, he pleads guilty. Given a fine, Burton says that he cannot pay, and looks to be facing prison time; but the lenient magistrate determines that, if he's taken back to the holding cell for another day, this will be punishment enough.

It sounds like a lucky let-off, but Burton isn't pleased with the outcome. He's furious. Because Burton isn't Burton. He's George Orwell, the novelist. He's made up the whole Burton backstory and deliberately caused a disturbance because he wants to go to prison.

Orwell went on to become one of the most famous and successful novelists of all time, creating lasting classics like *1984* and *Animal Farm*, and also inventing concepts and phrases like "Cold War", "Big Brother" and "thoughtcrime" that still resonate today.

One of the secrets of his success was his painstaking attention to detail and in-depth research. He wanted to go to prison because he wanted to *write about* prison and didn't feel he could do the job properly without first-hand experience. (Although, in this case, admittedly, he had to make do with his holding-cell experience.)

I am not suggesting you need to go to prison – or indulge in similar "method acting" devices – to make your writing authentic. But I am suggesting that you note Orwell's commitment to deep research. This is one of several ideas that you can usefully learn from Orwell as we explore the realities of the writing process.

Understanding a few "trade secrets" can help you improve your writing

For most people at work, writing is not their primary skill. It is one of those additional skills, like presenting and managing upwards, which at some point you realise has become part of your job, alongside the more basic skills that you need to fulfil the specific requirements of your role. However, just as with presenting and managing upwards, it is a vital skill for career success.

Many colleagues will conclude that somebody who cannot write clearly cannot think clearly either, that their muddled writing is evidence of muddled mental processes. This is untrue and unfair. However, as it is a reasonably common perception, improving your writing and your ability to communicate with others through the written word will not only help you to refine your storytelling but will have many other broader benefits as well.

One of the reasons that people believe they're not very good at writing is they misunderstand what the writing process is, and they assume that those people who write well also write effortlessly. When they write a poor first draft, they conclude that they are not skilled at writing, failing to understand that professional writers' first drafts are usually unimpressive too.

Some people undoubtedly have a natural talent for writing but, as in most areas of work, talent is only one of the necessary elements; hard work and an understanding of the correct process are equally important.

Even most professional writers do not have a natural talent for instantly thinking of the right word, the happiest phrase or the perfect structure. Writing is an iterative process that takes time and that benefits from patience and persistence.

As someone who is regularly asked to rewrite presentations, documents and speeches, I have grown used to the request to "sprinkle your magic on this". There is no magic. The process by which the writing is improved takes more effort than "sprinkling".

This chapter looks at the specific aspects of writing that professional writers know but those who are only occasionally called upon to write may not realise. Understanding these "trade secrets" will help those for whom writing is not a natural talent to maximise the clarity and effectiveness of their writing, while helping them to avoid the most common writing mistakes.

They can be summarised using the handy acronym AUTHOR.

Analogue: Start with paper and pens, not Word or PowerPoint.

Understand: Know your audience and what they want.

Talk: Write the same way you speak.

Headlines: Write all your headlines first.

One: Keep to one point per slide or paragraph.

Rewrite: Writing is rewriting.

The good news is that you can always improve your writing skills. The less good news is that it will take a little bit of work.

Analogue: start with paper and pens, not Word or PowerPoint

Your writing medium affects your writing, and you should therefore choose carefully how you approach the physical act of writing.

Writing, like most creative pursuits, consists of two very different stages: a divergent stage and a convergent stage. In the former, you explore ideas; in the latter, you move in a more focused way towards an end product.

In the divergent stage, while exploring different options, the analogue world of paper and pens, sticky notes and different coloured pens or crayons is more effective. The digital world, meanwhile, has advantages as an executional medium that make it the natural partner for the convergent stage when the focus is on an outcome.

There have been a number of research studies monitoring brain activity to compare the overall effectiveness of using paper and pens with digital devices for various tasks. And it seems that almost everybody, even digital natives, benefits from beginning their writing process in the analogue medium, using paper and pens or pencils rather than staring at a computer.

Studies conducted at the University of Tokyo which placed respondents in fMRI brain scanners showed that significantly more brain activity is involved in writing with a pen than in typing on a keyboard.[1] This robust brain activity and the activation of multiple brain regions seems to help both the encoding and retrieval of information and in turn appears to help people make connections between ideas as they create and structure presentations and documents. They are simply more in control of the information. They understand it on a deeper level and can do more with it.

The research calls out the benefits of "highlighting, underlining, circling, drawing arrows, handwriting, colour coded notes in the margins" and other techniques more intuitively and easily applied using pens and paper. The researchers have theorised that it is "the complex spatial and tactile information associated with writing by hand on physical paper" that makes the process superior to the "uniform scrolling up and down and standardised arrangement of text" in the digital domain.

Longitudinal studies by psychologist Virginia Berninger have emphasised that people are also able to express more ideas more quickly when using pen and paper than when working in a digital medium.[2]

Writing with a pen or pencil on paper is a fundamentally different activity from typing. It uses more of the brain. It encodes the information deeper in the brain, but also leaves it more accessible, allowing the free flow of ideas and the making of connections that is vital to creative writing.

Clearly, we are not going to stem the tide of the digital world, and the many advantages of digital media in terms of efficiency and scalability mean that most work will remain in that sphere. However, it's definitely worth retaining the skill of writing with a pen on paper as an alternative to typing on a keyboard for certain tasks.

Certainly, when you are at the early stages of a creative process, you will achieve better results in the analogue world. When writing, it is only at the later stages as you focus down on the precise word or phrase and the exact structure that the executional advantages of digital media make it your preferred option.

In the early stages, the digital medium is not just unhelpful; it is actively working against you. The first stage of writing is not outcome based. You are not trying to get to the end product. You are trying to explore the territory, examine different possibilities and experiment. But if you work in, for example, PowerPoint, you will be pushed towards solutions too quickly. The temptation to cut and paste slides from a previous presentation is too great for most people to resist.

It's so simple. It's so quick. And you get the sense of having written something, having made progress. But in fact you haven't, because what you have done will not help you build your story.

Making things simple and quick is exactly what most software is designed to do; it removes what people in the software world refer to as "friction". Unfortunately, the "friction" makes writing better. The struggle to make sense of ideas and find the right shape for the story *is* the writing process, not a problem that occurs in the process that needs to be removed. By removing it, software makes writing seemingly easier ... but worse.

The most creative stage – the divergent stage – of the writing process is better served if you are allowed to wander around, having ideas that may be appropriate at different stages of the story in whatever order they occur to you rather than moving too quickly to a finished structure.

One of the most important advantages of this "friction" has been highlighted by the author Neil Gaiman, who said that he loves "the fact that handwriting *forces* you to do a second draft, rather than just tidying up and deleting bits on a computer". (My italics.)

Since you can't present your work formally without moving it into the digital medium, starting in analogue does indeed necessitate a second draft – thereby ensuring that you do not make the mistake of thinking that writing is a one-draft process. The second draft is vital. And we'll come back to that when we get to the letter "R" of AUTHOR.

The analogue medium also gives you access to your earlier thoughts. If you have an idea in Word or PowerPoint, change your mind and delete it, it's gone. Although you can undo your commands to a certain extent, in all practical terms the previous (now out of favour) idea has been removed from your vision and your awareness and will not come back. Ideas that have been scribbled on paper remain. Even as you decide to move a paragraph further down by circling it and placing an arrow to its new location, the possibility of it moving back or even moving somewhere else remains open at all times. All your thought processes for the whole phase of work are available to you. They stay on the page and they stay workable. They can be questioned. They can be revised.

When you are writing in a group, working in the analogue medium offers the further advantage that it is far easier to collaborate in a meaningful and inclusive way. The cliché of a group of people scribbling on Post-its and slapping them on a wall has become a cliché precisely because it works so well. Although digital equivalents might seem to replicate the experience – and sometimes there'll be no option other than to use them – the physical nature of this interaction, the democratic nature of the process, is beautifully suited to the divergent phase of creativity.

Even as you move into the later stages of the writing process, when you should be in the digital world, group collaboration has to be handled very carefully. The usual default – shared documents – is often a recipe for disaster. When everybody is allowed to access a shared document and modify it, with everybody effectively working on one version of one document, the result will tend to be that each individual starts their editing from a "what do I want to say?" place, which (as explained in Chapter 3) is exactly the wrong place to start. You end up with a cumbersome, confused, over-elaborate document full of stuff that simply shouldn't be there.

At this later stage of the writing process, one person has to be the "author" of the work and retain control of what goes in, what comes out and what moves around, otherwise the integrity of your story will inevitably be compromised.

Yes, this is a slightly less convenient, slightly more difficult way of working, but once again the "friction" in the process is what makes the results better.

You may feel resistance – or you may experience resistance from colleagues – to the idea of working in the analogue medium because of concerns about wasting the resources of the planet or contributing to climate change. It would obviously be inappropriate to use paper for tasks where it is not needed, or to use paper wastefully. However, the power consumption of working in the digital domain – laptops, tablets, phones, servers – and the largely hidden lifecycle of electronic devices, from production through powering to disposal, is at least as damaging as using paper, if not more so.[3] Wasting paper is of course something we should always avoid. But using paper wisely for those moments at work where it is the most appropriate tool remains a sensible option.

Understand: know your audience and what they want

One of the most important themes in this book is that the subject of your story should be your audience, not yourself. This involves knowing as much as possible about them. How much? Well, perhaps don't go to quite the lengths that George Orwell did, but do be inspired by his dedication to the task.

I repeat this idea here because, when you begin writing (even when you have previously done a lot of research into the audience), it's very easy to revert to a self-centred viewpoint during the actual writing process. As you sit with a pen in your hand there is a natural tendency to return to the sort of questions – "What do I want to say?" and "How do I want to say it?" – that propel you back to a self-focused place.

It's entirely natural to ask yourself these questions when you're writing, so it's vital that you actively counter their effect by researching your audience not as a separate activity, but as an integral part of the writing process itself. As you're writing, you should review your knowledge of your audience and extend it if necessary. If there are gaps in it which you think you can fill, take the time (wherever possible) to do this.

This maximises the chances that your writing will answer the crucial question that your audience will apply to it: "What's in it for me?"

Mike Nichols, the film and theatre director, once noted: "The audience asks 'Why are you telling me this?' and you have to have an answer. ... The answer is: 'This is about you. This is about your life. The life we all have together.' And if you do it right, they will say 'Yes! How did you know?'"

This is the effect you want the story you are telling to have. You want the audience to feel "Yes! This person is talking about me, my company, my challenges, my opportunities."

If, as you write, you find yourself stuck, wondering exactly how to best express an idea, stop asking yourself "What do I say?" and instead work backwards to ask yourself "What does the audience want or need to hear at this point?" If you don't know, then you need to channel your inner George Orwell and do more research.

For example, consider your audience's demographics, their background, their interests. Establish what matters to them as individuals and what matters to them given their role in the company and the situation the company finds itself in within its market. Make a frank and honest assessment of your audience's knowledge of the topic you are discussing. You need to get the balance right: you do not want to bore them with a lot of information that they may already know but equally you do not want to confuse them with ideas they cannot be expected to understand.

Where possible, spend time getting to know your audience personally. Meet with them, talk to them, ask them questions. If this isn't possible, find other people who have spent time with them and talk to *them*. Who else do you know who may have met them before?

These days this task is easier than ever before. Companies' websites and social media will tell you a huge amount about their culture, values, mission, products, services and customers. And most individuals will have an online and social media presence, which you can access to help you understand them both within the professional roles and as people.

Investigate their competition. What are other companies in their sector like? What are they doing the same and what are they doing differently?

Reach back to find examples of when you have communicated with similar companies or similar individuals: what worked and what didn't.

Be absolutely clear about the intended outcome of your communication. What are the outcomes you expect? What are the emotional needs that you need to meet to move your audience towards this outcome?

Talk: write the same way you speak

When writing work documents and presentations, using short words and simple language is better than using technical terms, jargon and long words. Simple sentences are better than complex sentences. Simple, short paragraphs are better than long, meandering paragraphs. As George Orwell wrote: "Never use a long word where a short one will do."

Unless you work in the legal profession or academia or in a culture where there is a carefully prescribed form of written communication, it's best to forget any idea that there is a special, more formal approach to writing which involves using a vocabulary or constructions that you would not normally use when talking. You should write the same way you speak.

Orwell also counsels against using technical jargon. It's a good idea to rid yourself of the thought that using long words, complicated sentences and lots of technical jargon will add to your authority or credibility with your audience. Quite the opposite. The respect that you show to an audience by using language that they will easily understand increases your credibility and authority. Even though Albert Einstein probably never said these words often attributed to him – "If you can't explain something to a six-year-old, you don't understand it yourself" – there is an implicit truth in the statement. Someone fully in command of a subject is able to talk about it using familiar words so that others can easily grasp it. The person who leans heavily on long words and technical jargon is likely revealing not a depth of knowledge, but a superficial and shaky understanding of a subject.

William Strunk and E. B. White in their classic text on writing, *The Elements of Style*, make this point with a helpful analogy. "Vigorous writing is concise. A sentence should contain no unnecessary words, a paragraph no unnecessary sentences, for the same reason that a drawing should have no unnecessary lines and a machine no unnecessary parts."[4] Adding unnecessary extra components to a machine does not make it more efficient. The same is true of a piece of communication.

There is a second meaning to the word *talk* in the AUTHOR model. Once you have a draft that you are reasonably satisfied with, say it out loud.

Nothing can expose the potential flaws in a piece of writing as quickly and accurately as having to read it out. It will help you to identify errors, locate awkward sentences and find any areas where your writing is not clear. It will help you to improve the rhythm and pace of what you write, to hear how the words work together and whether they sound natural. You will also become viscerally aware of any sentences that are too long, repetitive or complicated because they will be hard for you to read out loud.

You will also gain a sense of whether your writing is in the correct order because when you review a text without reading it out, you can mentally skip forwards and backwards, providing additional context to yourself. When you are forced to slow down and read something out loud, you hear each word and sentence in its place – and can note when it doesn't work there.

Headlines: write all your headlines first

When you think you're ready to write your first draft, stop. Instead, write a series of headlines. If what you're writing is a presentation, then you are simply writing the headlines to each slide. If you're writing a document these headlines are the key sentences that will appear in the text, your main points.

Working in this way will ensure that your writing does indeed contain the main points you want to make, that you stay true to your overall story and that you do not get lost and meander away from the point.

It's vital that you get this simplified version of your overall story clear in your mind before you write all the text, because otherwise it's all too easy to get lost in the detail. The legendary film director Billy Wilder offered this simple advice to writers: "Know where you're going." Starting with your headlines ensures that you do.

It's important that you write the right kind of headline. The type of headlines you want – storytelling headlines – are explained in Chapter 4.

A storytelling headline makes your key point in language that you would speak out loud and will usually express a clear benefit to your audience. There are at least two other kinds of headlines that you are likely to encounter regularly: they are doing different jobs and are constructed differently. It's important that you do not use these kinds of headlines, so let's be very clear about the differences.

Newspaper headlines follow a style that was developed when print was the only medium and are designed to fit into specific, unalterable spaces. Historically, it would be normal practice for one person to design the page, defining the font size of the headline, the length of each column line and the number of lines available for a headline, and then for another journalist to write the headline keeping precisely to these parameters. As a result, newspaper headlines use a lot of shorthand techniques just to make headlines fit which we in our storytelling headlines absolutely want to avoid. Newspaper headlines leave out any words that they can – words like "a" and "the" and "is" and "her" – and we need to keep these words in our headlines so that we are using storytelling language.

The other headline we do not want to emulate is the typical online clickbait headline that promises that you will be "amazed" by "this one weird trick". You do not want a series of headlines that promise something amazing or wonderful that never occurs.

This technique is effective in providing a series of dopamine hits to the bored, casually scrolling internet user but will leave your audience annoyed and disappointed.

One: keep to one point per slide or paragraph

One of the most common and glaring flaws in written business documents is a lack of any paragraph discipline. Paragraphs wander on and on, creating long blocks of text that are forbidding just to look at and confusing if the reader tries to tackle them.

Each paragraph of a document, and each slide of a presentation, should be about one thing and one thing only. When you change subject, you should move on to a new slide or a new paragraph. Adherence to this rule adds clarity to your writing and helps your audience to follow the flow of your story.

Everyone knows what a slide is, but perhaps not everyone

is entirely sure what a paragraph is – or rather, why writers choose to end one paragraph and begin a new one.

A paragraph is a collection of sentences that revolve around one single idea. The first sentence of your paragraph should be similar to the headline of your slide. It should state the most important idea of the paragraph as clearly as possible.

The rest of the paragraph then supports this single idea. The subsequent sentences in the paragraph can perform several roles: they can explain or clarify any points in the first sentence; they can provide evidence that supports the main idea, providing data, quotes or research that back it up; they can provide illustrative examples. However, once you wish to move on to the next point or subject, you need a new paragraph.

Rewrite: writing is rewriting

There's probably more time wasted in wondering how to start than in any other part of the writing process. It's wasted because the answer is: just start anywhere. Agonising over your opening sentence or opening slide at the beginning of the process is pointless, because you will come back and rewrite it anyway.

The novelist Joyce Carol Oates said: "The first sentence can't be written until the final sentence is written." This may not be literally true, but it is certainly the case that you will have a better idea of what your opening should be when you are much further into the writing process.

It isn't just your opening that will get rewritten. One of the most common pieces of advice given to writers is that "writing is rewriting", and that is absolutely true. No matter how talented a writer you are, do not expect to write a first draft and leave it at that.

It can be helpful to look online at the images widely available of the first typewritten draft of George Orwell's novel 1984 and his written corrections.[5] Simply looking at the opening page reveals that this acclaimed and successful writer, in creating one of the best-known novels of all time, rejected considerably more than half of this section of his first draft when he went through again to revise. And these are corrections to the first *typewritten* draft; there may well have been much writing and rewriting before that.

If great writers are unhappy with their first draft, then you should not take the fact that *your* first draft isn't great yet as a sign of any failing on your part. This is what writing is like.

Rewriting allows you to rethink your structure, to reorganise ideas, develop points more fully, support your claims better, address counter arguments, make sure that the work is consistent in tone, that transitions between slides or paragraphs make sense and that the overall story flow has survived intact.

Rewriting can involve adding more text, cutting text, moving text around or changing words and phrases.

Usually, the temptation is to add material, but in fact it's cutting that is often the best tactic at this stage – however hard it is to do. If that fancy phrase that you're so pleased with doesn't move the story forward, it has to go. Although it can be painful, try to follow the vividly expressed advice of the novelist Stephen King: "Kill your darlings, kill your darlings, even when it breaks your egocentric little scribbler's heart, kill your darlings."

Earlier I discussed the benefits of reading an early draft out loud to yourself to catch any obvious errors. Once you have a more advanced draft, when you are starting to think that perhaps the work is finished, try reading it out loud to a colleague. Any issues in the work will quickly be identified as you will find yourself wanting to correct them as you go along. You will notice the vast majority of errors yourself just before you read them out, as you will instinctively want to stop reading whenever you reach any moments of clumsiness or overcomplication in your writing.

Editing other people's work ... without crushing their spirit

As well as creating your own content, you may be charged with giving feedback on other people's writing, helping them to edit their communications and tell their stories.

The tricky part here is improving their work without either simply imposing your views on them or hurting their feelings and damaging their self-esteem by being overly critical.

Faced with a piece of writing from a team member that you know is not good enough, how can you raise the quality of the work without lowering the morale of the person responsible for it? Apart from being an unpleasant experience for the individual involved, this may also be bad for business as perhaps that individual will have to present the work soon after the feedback session. You need them to believe both in it and in themselves.

The best solution to this delicate problem is to use an editing model. This will allow you and the original author to compare their work against an objective set of criteria rather than get into a subjective "This isn't good enough" type of conversation.

One example is *Do Think Feel*, a simple model in which you ask "What do we want the audience to do/think/feel when they see this slide/read this paragraph?" and answer it together, checking that this objective is achieved.

You will find that often the author will correct their own work in this process, rather than you having to criticise or amend it.

A variation of this, which we first met in Chapter 6, is *The Slide/Paragraph Where They* ... This model is especially useful when a piece of work is being produced by many authors or where feedback has been absorbed from many stakeholders. Using *The Slide/Paragraph Where They* ..., the team aligns around a simple statement for each slide (or paragraph), along the lines of:

"This is the slide/paragraph where they ... see how poor the customer experience is in their stores"

"This is the slide/paragraph where they ... understand how well our tech stack fits with theirs"

"This is the slide/paragraph where they ... are reassured that we will offer 24/7 support throughout the project"

It is always "This is the slide/paragraph where *they* ...", never "This is the slide where *we* ...".

Once you agree on what comes after the three dots, you can decide together whether the slide achieves this objective. As with *Do Think Feel*, this removes the sense of personal criticism from the process.

When models like these are used sensitively and transparently ("I want to sense-check your work against this model, which is sometimes helpful" rather than "This needs a lot of work"), it allows the original author (or authors) to enter into a process of discovery with the editor, rather than just sitting there being criticised or told what to do.

Find the right time and place to write (whenever possible)

Although it's important to be realistic and acknowledge that writing projects come with a deadline and many of those deadlines are tight, it is worth stating that most people do have a time and place in which they do their best writing.

This doesn't mean that you can always get to write in your perfect environment or at your ideal time, but it helps to know what your "perfect world" set-up is, so that you can function at your best whenever it's possible and get as close as you can to that ideal environment on other occasions.

You probably have a strong sense of your body clock. If possible, think about shifting the admin tasks into the lower energy phase of your day, so that you can write when you are at your most alert. It's also important to spend some time asking yourself: what is your ideal writing space? Can you write at your desk – the same desk where you do all your other work – or are you better when you move to another location? Do you write well with some background music or do you prefer silence? Do you need to be intensely focused on your work or do you produce better results when there are occasional interruptions from colleagues?

There is no right answer for any of these. We're all different. The important thing is to know what works for you. Then try to create as positive an environment as you can for your writing while not allowing yourself to start to believe that you can *only* write under those circumstances. Your writing, like so much else at work, will sometimes be a compromise.

If there's one overall lesson of this chapter it is that writing, like so many things, is a mixture of talent, hard work and understanding the right process. Following a process like the one outlined above and devoting an appropriate amount of time to the writing task will lead to great results.

10

The stories you need to know

Identifying your personal stories through self-discovery; and how to build the five vital stories that you need to be able to tell about your organisation

The Greek philosopher Socrates once met with a wealthy young man known as Euthydemus the Handsome. With a nickname like that you will hardly be surprised to learn that Euthydemus was a bit arrogant. He was known for collecting the works of the great philosophers and poets, and for assuming that he had absorbed their wisdom and would make a great statesman.

Socrates, never easily impressed, decided to find out just how wise Euthydemus really was. He subjected the young man to a long line of questions about truth and lies, justice and injustice, knowledge and ignorance. Finally, he asked him whether he had ever visited the Temple of Apollo at Delphi, a revered and sacred site.

Euthydemus said that he had. Twice. And had he, Socrates asked, happened to notice the inscription on the wall of the temple that read simply "Know thyself"? Euthydemus had noticed it. Socrates wondered what the young man made of this suggestion made at such an important – and indeed divinely connected – place. Had he bothered to do anything about it? Had he sought to know himself better?

"Indeed I did not," Euthydemus answered, "because I felt sure that I knew that already; for I could hardly know anything else if I did not even know myself."

You do not need to be a student of ancient Greek literature (the dialogue is recounted in Xenophon's *Memorabilia*) or a philosopher yourself to get the drift. We know that Euthydemus is misguided here. We know that Socrates will go on to explain to him in some detail that he doesn't know himself at all, and that he should heed the words written on the temple wall.

There were in fact two other inscriptions at Delphi: "Nothing in excess" and "Surety brings ruin". Both are helpful credos in the modern world of work, but it is "Know thyself" which has most resonated down the ages, and which concerns us now.

It's your turn now

A continuing theme of this book has been the idea that you should never be the hero of your story – that the hero of your story should always be your audience, whether that be your team, your customers, or another organisation.

This has been emphasised throughout the book because of the fundamental human tendency to do the exact opposite – to talk about oneself.

Having done everything I can to steer you away from that human tendency, the time has now come to concede that, on occasions, you do need to tell your own story.

Bearing in mind everything that has been said so far, you will always aim to tell your story in a way that ensures that it resonates with your audience, and that they can see that this is *their story too*. But yes, sometimes you need to tell your own story – either your personal story, or that of your organisation.

This chapter outlines the process you need to go through to understand your stories, your team's stories and your organisation's stories. This involves gaining a deeper understanding of yourself and your organisation. The second part of the chapter then builds on this general discovery process by outlining the specific stories that are most commonly told at work:

An origins story

A vision story

A story about overcoming challenges

A story about navigating change

A story about values.

Doing the general discovery work and then understanding these specific stories in relation to yourself, your organisation and your stakeholders will help make all your communications to internal and external audiences more powerful.

Even if you never actually stand up in front of an audience and tell these stories or write them down, understanding them and understanding how they shape you and the organisation will improve your work. It will give a clarity to your actions and your strategic prioritisation; you will have a clearer understanding of what you do and why.

Indeed, the process of self-discovery necessary to unearth your stories is, in itself, a valuable discipline.

Who are you?

Before you can tell your stories, you need to know your stories. Before you can talk about yourself, you need to know yourself.

"Know thyself" wasn't only an important idea in ancient Greek civilisation. The idea that it is beneficial to look more deeply within ourselves has been repeated within the great religions and wisdom traditions – Christianity, Islam, Buddhism, Confucianism – through to the philosophy of Nietzsche and the working methods of Freud and Jung. And in modern emotional intelligence theory, self-awareness or self-knowing, and consequently self-management, are considered core skills.

The better you understand yourself, the better you will function at work and in life generally. So, it's inadvisable to take Euthydemus's approach of "*Of course* I know myself". Instead, take the time to dig a little deeper.

If you have worked closely with a coach or a therapist, you may already have embarked on a journey of self-discovery. But many people have never actively done so. One reason may be that it simply sounds so daunting, and in a sense it is. The process of self-discovery can go deep and is arguably a project that *could* take your entire life.

However, while many people might prefer not to take such a lengthy or cathartic journey, *any* level of self-discovery can be helpful. Everyone can benefit from setting aside time to answer a few simple questions about themselves – and taking time to reflect on the answers they come up with.

To understand your story, answer the following questions

When are you most yourself?

Take a period of time, say a week, and at the end of each day note the times during that day, both at work and out of work, when you felt most yourself. When did you feel most authentic? When were you happiest? When were you doing exactly what you wanted to be doing?

At the end of the week, review your notes and see if any themes emerge. What is it that's going on when you really feel that you are most yourself?

What does this tell you about your personality, about your

values and priorities, about what you want to do with your life and how you want to do it?

Who is the authentic you?

What are you good at?

Some of us are too modest to claim our achievements. Some of us simply don't think about it. Others have a tendency to feel that if they can do something, then it can't be that big a deal.

Cast all your modesty aside and spend some time writing down exactly what you are good at.

Identify some examples over the past few years where you've had personal success. They could be successes at work or at home or in your wider community. They don't need to be successes that others have recognised (although include those too); if *you* felt a sense of achievement, that's a success.

Again, look to establish whether there are any common themes.

Think about the particular skills and talents you have. Are you good at any sport? Are you good at maths? Can you speak several languages? What kind of thinking are you good at? Are you a great problem-solver or do you have fantastic attention to detail? What are your craft skills? What training have you had?

Do you have any particular people skills? Are you good at motivating teams or calming down people who are under pressure?

What challenges have you faced?

Cast your mind back to the key struggles of your life and career. What were the challenges? What were the moments when you faced challenges or barriers that seemed so daunting that perhaps, at first, they seemed they would prove too much for you?

How did you overcome them? What were the resources you called on? What were the skills you used? Who were the allies who helped you?

What did you learn about yourself during the process? Did you unearth any talents that you didn't realise you had? Did you adjust your view of your potential or what is possible in the world? Did you adjust your view of the world around you?

What motivates you?

Write down a list of the things that motivate you and try to rank them to establish which are the most important to you. If the question "What motivates you?" is hard to answer, try wording it in other ways.

For example: what activities are most important to you? What gets you out of bed in the morning? What do you really enjoy doing? What would you do even if you weren't paid to do it? What gives you a feeling of fulfilment?

People can be motivated by a wide range of factors. These could include monetary reward, promotion, recognition, a simple thank-you, learning, helping others, enjoying an intellectual challenge or just having autonomy over your work.

If you are struggling to answer the question, try thinking instead about occasions where you have felt very *unmotivated* or frustrated. What led to that feeling? The opposite of that is probably one of your motivators.

Where are you going?

Spend some time thinking about your goals and ambitions. If you don't have specific goals, think instead of your general direction of travel. Where are you heading?

What do you think is the next step in your career? Where do

you want to be in five years' time? Where do you want to be in ten years' time?

How close are you to where you thought you would be? If you seem to be nowhere near your original intentions, have you veered off course or have you made sensible pragmatic adjustments as life has thrown you new challenges?

Do you plan to pursue a vertical career moving upwards in your current area, or to have a T-shaped career zigzagging through different areas, sectors and skill sets? Do you envisage yourself changing jobs frequently? Moving abroad?

How do you make a difference?

Make a list of the ways you currently make a difference at work and in your personal life, and ways in which you *could* make a difference.

Ask yourself: who benefits from what you're doing? How do you make situations better? How do you have a positive impact on your organisation and on people around you? Who benefits directly from what you do and who benefits indirectly?

How do you make a difference to individuals in your team, your customers and clients, family members and friends? And how are your actions making a positive contribution to society and to the planet?

Others can help you unearth your story

You may choose to go through the above questions alone or you may choose to go through the questions with a buddy who is also interested in developing their storytelling.

This will be a choice based on your personality. Some people like to do work like this on their own. Others feel that they gain from an outside perspective. There's no right answer – only the answer that seems right to you.

Although the phrase "first thought, best thought" is sometimes true, it is usually a good idea with work like this to allow time for reflection. Answer the questions. Leave them for a few days. Come back and re-assess them. In the meantime, ideas will have bubbled up from your unconscious and you can refine your answers.

Focus on people, places and moments that matter

If you get stuck for an answer, the way to uncover more meaning is to focus on people, places and moments. This allows you to approach the work from a different angle, which you might find more productive.

Ask yourself: who are the people who really matter to you? They could be family members, friends, colleagues, inspirational figures from the past, or people who influence you today.

Why are they important? What do you derive from the relationship? Why does the relationship matter?

Deep dive into thoughts of places that matter in your life to allow memories to surface. Where were you? Why was this place important? What was happening?

Isolate the moments that were the key turning points in your life. What were the moments in your life when "nothing would ever be the same" afterwards?

How to tell the most difficult story

You can use the information that surfaces from the above questions to help you construct many different stories about yourself.

Whatever the story, always remember to look for parallels

between yourself and your audience. This is particularly tricky when you're faced with the simple but daunting interview question (whether in a formal interview process, or in an informal conversation): "Tell me/us a little about yourself."

This is perhaps the most difficult storytelling moment you will face. Given such a broad question, many people just start waffling. So how do you narrow down this widest of briefs to create a cohesive narrative? And how do you obey the most basic storytelling rule – that your story must resonate with your audience – when you've been told specifically to make the story about you?

The following table shows you how.

Act	What happens in a good story	The SUPERB process	How to apply the SUPERB process to the "Tell us about yourself" story
One	The audience is made to identify strongly with the hero	*Shared experiences*	Even if you have been asked specifically to talk about yourself, begin by aligning yourself with your audience. Reference some way in which your story is similar to other people's stories
	The audience understands what quest the hero is on and what their destination is	*Ultimate triumph*	At this point, the audience must understand what success looks like for you – the vision that drives you forward, the dreams you had as a child or perhaps early in your career (and these must connect in some way with your current reality). Present these ambitions in a way that acknowledges their similarities to the dreams and ambitions of others
Two	The hero meets a major challenge, and decides to take it on	*Problem definition*	The audience must be clear about what challenges you faced. Wherever possible find the universal in these challenges – something that others can relate to

	The hero successfully overcomes the challenge	*Explore options ...*	The audience must be clear about how you overcame these challenges. Include some false starts or wrong moves and subsequent course-correction. No one gets it right all the time
	The hero faces successive, more difficult challenges, and overcomes them usually with the help of allies	*... and objections*	Don't exaggerate your challenges, and acknowledge that others have faced similar (and harder) challenges
Three	To prepare to overcome the hardest challenge, the hero has to see themselves and/or the world in a new way	*Real*	Explain how – in tackling these challenges – you learned something new about yourself, or gained a new perspective on life, work, relationships or all of them. If these learnings are very specific to the task, find a way to express them in more general terms. (So your learning isn't "Janice from accounts knows everybody"; it's "building informal networks in the organisation can be beneficial")
	The hero succeeds	*Best of both worlds*	End in a place where you are successful (in the broadest sense), but where others have benefited too

Having applied this clear storytelling structure to the vague and therefore daunting "Tell us about yourself" question, you will find it easier to go through the same process to build stories in answer to more focused briefs and questions.

You can do similar preparatory work on your team's story or your organisation's story ...

You can apply the same questions to your team or your organisation as a way of gaining greater understanding.

When is your team/organisation at its best?

What is your team/organisation good at?

What drives and motivates your team/organisation?

Where is your team/organisation going? What are its short-, medium- and long-term goals?

How does your team/organisation make a difference?

... and on your customer's/client's/audience's story

Throughout the book I have championed the importance of understanding your audience when telling your story, whether that audience is your own people, your customers and clients or another organisation to whom you are pitching or presenting.

You can modify the questions above to develop another way of understanding these audiences.

How does your audience see themselves?

What is your audience good at?

What do you think motivates your audience?

What does your audience want in the short, medium and long term?

How does your audience believe that they can make a difference in the world?

Here's how to write the stories that matter most

Having done this general discovery work, it's now time to look at the stories you are most likely to need when communicating with your people, customers and other stakeholders at work:

an origins story, a vision story, a story about overcoming challenges, a story about navigating change and a story about values.

In each case, I outline the key questions you need to answer before you can write the story, suggest a source of inspiration from a famous business leader, and highlight a classical storytelling structure that you can borrow.

The classical storytelling structures are taken from Christopher Booker's book *The Seven Basic Plots*.[1] In this, Booker expanded upon the hero's journey, which we looked at in Chapter 2 – and which Booker terms "the meta-plot", dividing it into seven different variations.

Three of these, which he called *Comedy, Tragedy* and *Rags to Riches,* are not useful for our current purposes, but you can borrow ideas from the four others as you tell your organisation's stories. These are:

The Quest

Overcoming the Monster

Voyage and Return

Rebirth

An origin story

Why this story matters

One of the most important stories for anyone to know is their organisation's origin story. Telling stories about your organisation's origins can be a powerful way to inspire your team, to onboard new people and to connect with potential customers or clients. It helps all these groups to understand what is important about your company.

Ask these questions to uncover your story

How did your organisation begin?

What need among your customers or stakeholders did your organisation meet?

Who recognised this need and how did they recognise it?

When your organisation started, how was it different from others in the sector?

What were some of the challenges of the early days of your organisation?

How did it overcome those challenges?

What were the learnings from this time and how do they impact the organisation today?

What was true and important in the early days that remains true and important for the organisation today?

When your organisation is functioning at its best, how does this relate back to the organisation's origins?

Be inspired by this business leader's story

In his book *Onward*, Howard Schultz, the CEO of Starbucks, tells the story about a trip he took to Milan, a year after he joined Starbucks, where he was inspired by Italy's coffee culture – the way that coffee shops in the city were not just places to grab a cup of coffee on the go, but formed an important part of the community.[2] He saw an opportunity to bring this sense of place and of community to Starbucks, creating the "third place" between work and home.

You can find a short summary of this in an online interview with Schultz, where he explains how, in Italy, he experienced "the sense of community and romance and theatre around espresso".[3] Back in the United States he explained the idea to the firm's founders – who rejected it. Schultz left the company, but later was able to buy Starbucks and implement his ideas.

Borrow from this classic plot

A company's origin story fits most closely to *The Quest*. This is the nearest of Christopher Booker's plots to the hero's journey (see Chapter 2 if you need a quick refresher on this).

In *The Quest*, the hero is on a relentless quest to attain an all-important goal. The hero meets many obstacles and barriers but also finds allies who will provide support. Examples in fiction include *The Iliad*, *The Lord of the Rings*, *Raiders of the Lost Ark* and *The Avengers* films.

Adapt it like this

In your version, the quest is on behalf of the audience that you're communicating to.

There is something your audience needed that they could not get. Your organisation overcame challenges to fulfil this need. There were more conflicts and challenges along the way as the organisation grew. There may have been temporary failures. There were also important learnings. Finally, the organisation succeeded in achieving its quest to fulfil the customer need, and as a result succeeded itself.

A mission story

Why this story matters

Telling stories about your organisation's mission can help to create a sense of purpose and direction for your people. It helps them to have a better understanding of how their individual efforts contribute to the company's overall goals. A mission story also helps you differentiate your company in the eyes of potential customers, clients and other stakeholders.

Ask these questions to uncover your story

What is the ultimate goal of the work you do?

How does your organisation's work benefit its customers and clients?

When your organisation successfully achieves its mission, how have individual customer's or client's lives changed? (Be as specific as possible.)

How does the organisation's work benefit society and the planet?

What other organisations have similar missions and how successful are they?

What are some examples of individual tasks or projects carried out by individuals or teams in your organisation that personify the mission?

What have you learned from pursuing your mission?

Be inspired by this business leader's story

Steve Jobs, co-founder and long-time leader of Apple, is often quoted as saying that he wanted the company to "make a dent in the universe". This language is cited in Walter Isaacson's excellent biography of Jobs, which is a fantastic if lengthy read to get a fix on Jobs's level of commitment towards his mission.[4] Alternatively, watch his commencement speech at Stanford University in 2005, in which he shares three stories that vividly explain his attitude to life and to his life's work.[5]

Borrow from this classic plot

An organisation's mission story fits also fits closely to *The Quest* (see the *Origin Story* section, above).

Adapt it like this

This is a rare instance where you *are* the hero of your story. You are on a quest to offer a new or different or improved product or service (the ultimate beneficiary of your quest is your audience). Your organisation will have to overcome many challenges to create this new product and service and you will need to find allies and to incorporate critical learnings along the way.

You can tell a mission story either as a guide to where you're going, or as a story of a mission achieved. However, if you choose the latter approach, there must be a sense of a further quest ahead – a need to reinvent or further improve the product or service. There should then be both a sense of completion and a sense of a restless need to progress.

A story about overcoming challenges

Why this story matters

A story about facing and overcoming challenges can help colleagues to understand that obstacles and setbacks are a normal part of the business process, that they can be overcome with the right attitude and processes and mindset, and that you can emerge stronger on the other side of the challenge.

Ask these questions to uncover your story

What challenges has your organisation faced?

When did your organisation overcome a significant obstacle or achieve a goal that initially seemed daunting?

What were the feelings that individuals experience during this moment?

What were some significant episodes or moments in the struggle to overcome – and the eventual triumph over – the challenges?

What lessons did the organisation learn and how did it change as a result of the struggle?

Who were the key individuals involved, and how did they contribute? How were they changed by the process?

Be inspired by this business leader's story

Sara Blakely, the founder and CEO of Spanx, created a billion-dollar business. But she had to overcome not only her own inner critic but external rejection and ridicule too. She has shared her story of persistence and her sense of humour that carried her through difficult times. Search for the candid interview that she gave to *Forbes* in 2012 or find other interviews with her on YouTube, including one on *The Insider Business Channel*: "If there's a failure or an 'oops' in your life, if you learn from it, and if you can laugh about it ... it's all worth it."[6]

Borrow from this classic plot

The story of overcoming challenges is similar to the classic structure of *Overcoming the Monster*. In this story, the protagonist has to defeat an evil and powerful monster that poses an immediate threat to them, their loved ones or their homeland.

Examples from fiction include *Beowulf, The War of the Worlds, Seven Samurai/The Magnificent Seven, Jaws* and the *Star Wars* franchise.

Adapt it like this

This is not a story of "Woe is me – I've had so many challenges in my life" nor is it a story of "Look at us – we're such heroes."

Although this *is* a heroic story of success, the part of the story that will resonate most strongly with your audience is the lessons that you learned from the struggle; what you learned about yourselves as individuals and as a team; and what tactics and strategy you learned were best placed to help you overcome the obstacles.

Look for takeaways that you can share with your audience that may be useful to them or may help to inspire them to tackle their own obstacles and achieve their own goals.

A story about navigating change

Why this story matters

Change is a constant in today's world of work; and it's important that you have a story that you can tell about the organisation's ability to navigate change and adapt to new situations. When identifying the story focus on a specific change that your company faced and how it came about.

Ask these questions to uncover your story

When was a time when your organisation needed to change? How did you know that change was necessary?

What needed to change within the organisation? (Thoughts? Beliefs? Behaviours? Attitudes? Processes? All of them?)

Were there any early attempts to make the change that failed? If so, why?

What was the catalyst/tipping point that finally made the change happen?

How was the change accomplished?

How did leaders in the organisation bring people along with the change?

How did certain individuals respond? Who stood out as an advocate of the change and who put the change into practice successfully?

Be inspired by this business leader's story

Jeff Bezos, the founder of Amazon, is one of the most successful business leaders of our time. With Amazon he has both responded to change and initiated change. Read his 2017 letter to shareholders, in which he shares the story about how Amazon has changed over the years: how it began as an online bookstore, grew into a massive global retailer, and has innovated constantly through its life.[7] Experimenting and trying new things have been important to the company, even if some of the experiments failed.

Borrow from this classic plot

A story about navigating change most closely echoes the classic plot *Voyage and Return*. In this kind of story, the protagonist voyages to (or sometimes just finds themselves in) a strange land. Initially they find it difficult to adapt to their new surroundings, but over time they learn important lessons about the new world, returning with new ways of thinking and behaving that help them in their life.

Examples of *Voyage and Return* in fiction include *Alice's Adventures in Wonderland*, *The Hobbit*, *Back to the Future* and *The Lion, the Witch and the Wardrobe*.

Adapt it like this

When you identify a story about change, focus on one specific change that your organisation faced and the steps that were taken to adapt to it.

Do not avoid any early failures or ignore the fact that it took the organisation a while to notice that change was necessary. Managing change is difficult and it's okay to acknowledge that in your story. However, also find the key players who helped move change forward and the moments that were critical in the change.

Again, focus on the lessons that were learned and takeaways that your audience can apply to their own work and lives.

A story about values

Why this story matters

Increasingly at work, doing something so that the company makes a profit and you make a salary is not enough.

Stakeholders, customers and shareholders are looking for companies that behave with clear values that help society and the planet. A story about values can help to communicate quickly how your organisation differentiates itself and what it stands for.

Ask these questions to uncover your story

What are your organisation's values? (Explain in a few sentences exactly what each value means to you.)

How does your organisation bring each of these values to life?

Who in your organisation exemplifies each of these values?

When your organisation fails to live up to its values, how does it respond?

Be inspired by this business leader's story

During her tenure as CEO of PepsiCo from 2006 to 2018, Indra Nooyi changed the business model, championing the concept of "performance and purpose". She has said that this was about asking the question "How can we keep performing while changing the portfolio to fundamentally improve the company's environmental footprint?"

Crucially, Nooyi said it was not a standalone corporate social responsibility programme, not a box-ticking exercise, but about "how we make money" – that performance and purpose are inextricably linked.

Check out her interview at the Stanford Graduate School of Business for a detailed explanation.[8]

Borrow from this classic plot

A story about values most closely echoes the classic plot *Rebirth*. In this story structure, an event forces the hero to change their behaviour and they become a better individual as a result.

Examples from fiction include *Beauty and the Beast*, *A Christmas Carol* and *Groundhog Day*.

Adapt it like this

Since conflict is at the heart of stories, the best kind of story about an organisation's values centres on an occasion when there was a fork in the road: when a company *could* have behaved in a way that went against its values but, with some sense of struggle or short-term sacrifice, instead lived up to its values and gained overall as a result.

You do not have to pretend that your company is squeaky clean, that everyone in the organisation always behaves at their absolute best. We are all human. Our values are there for us to aspire to and try to live up to and hopefully do live up to most of the time.

Understanding all these stories and being ready to tell them will enhance your communications skills, strengthen your personal brand, and help you to follow Socrates's advice that we should all heed the inscription at Delphi. You will indeed "know thyself" a bit better.

Epilogue

Sometimes an act of sabotage backfires.

Marpa was a spoilt rich kid. Born to a wealthy family in 11th-century Tibet, he terrorised the local area, drinking and fighting. Finally his parents gave in to the pressure from the locals and sent him to a Buddhist teacher to see if he could straighten him out.

Fortunately, Marpa took to Buddhism as fully as he had previously taken to drinking and fighting, quickly absorbed all that his teacher could pass onto him, and then he determined to seek out the original Buddhist teachings in India.

He cashed in his inheritance and used it to fund his travels. Over a period of many years, he visited over a hundred Buddhist masters, gained access to the most sacred teachings, translated them into his native language and set off for home, weighed down with a vast library of scrolls carrying the wisdom of centuries.

Marpa's one mistake was in his choice of travelling companion, Nyo. Another aspiring Buddhist teacher, Nyo was envious of Marpa's depth of learning. He decided that if he could just get rid of all the scrolls, then he not Marpa would be the greatest teacher in Tibet. So, as they crossed the river Ganges in a boat, Nyo hurled all the scrolls overboard.

Marpa returned home, thinking that his journey had been an abject failure ... but it turned out very differently.

For in all his discussions with the great Buddhist masters

Marpa had absorbed the *essence* of the teachings. The way forward was clear: Marpa would teach the key ideas of Buddhism based on what he had absorbed. The finer details contained in the lost scrolls scarcely mattered.

It worked. This broad-brush approach was the foundation of a school of the religion that is known as the Kagyu lineage, which survives today and has been extremely influential in the spread of Buddhist thought into the West. Envious Nyo is largely forgotten.

I am, obviously, not comparing the tips and techniques in this book with great spiritual teachings. But what I do want to suggest is that Marpa's approach – not to focus on every line of the ancient teachings but instead to convey the essence – can be helpful here.

There is great benefit to be had from strictly following the SUPERB storytelling model outlined in Chapter 5. The SUPERB model is a workplace Swiss army knife. It can be used to build stories and to edit presentations and documents, of course; but beyond that it can also help you to structure meetings, to navigate conversations, to give feedback, to enhance team-building activities and to maintain a customer-focused or audience-focused approach to your work. The more you use it, the more ways you will find to use it.

But in another sense – the Kagyu sense – the core of the book is not in the precise and exact structure of the SUPERB process. It is in the ideas that lie behind it. And if what you take from the book are these general ideas – the *essence* of storytelling – then you will also have gained knowledge that will benefit you greatly in work and in life.

So what are these core ideas? Let's summarise them here.

Story is extremely important ...

Stories help to explain why things are the way they are and (increasingly important in today's workplace) why things have to change. Stories are the most powerful way to persuade anybody to do anything.

... but not everything is a story

Most of life is not made up of stories and most of work is not made up of stories. As much as this book encourages you to use stories well, it encourages you to use them *sparingly*. Don't overuse the word "story "or bang on and on at work about how wonderful stories are. Simply introduce the ideas in this book into your work and your colleagues will come to see the benefits of the approach.

Alignment is crucial

In all your communications, getting on the same page as your audience is the sine qua non; if you don't do that, everything else you do becomes less effective. Always look to begin in a place of agreement.

Be clear on the quest

Before any communication (written or spoken) or any meeting, understand what it is you want to get out of the situation, but, much more importantly, understand what your audience needs to get out of it as well. This is the quest that will underpin a successful story.

Identify the challenges

Analyse the situation and discuss it to make sure that everyone involved agrees on what the challenges you are facing are, and the issues that need to be dealt with. Do not assume that everyone sees the problems in the same way or even sees the same problems. Before you can tell the right story, you need to ask a lot of questions.

There is rarely just one answer

It's always better to explore and discover solutions together rather than to work on the basis that you know the answer and nobody else does.

Anchor your ideas in reality

Try whenever possible to bring things back to the real lives of your audience. Stories are character driven. And unless people can see themselves and their everyday lives in your stories, your stories will not resonate with them.

Focus on your audience more than on your content

In all workplace communications, one of the most important lessons that storytelling can teach us is that the most important relationship is your relationship with your audience, not your relationship with your content. Spend more time thinking about your audience, their wants and needs than thinking about "What do I want to say?" Simply landing all your points is not good communication.

Storytelling is about connection

When a child asks a parent for one more story before the light is turned out, is it because the child is fascinated by plot and character and conflict and resolution? Or is it because they want to spend more time with someone who cares about them?

Even someone like me who teaches about plot and character

and conflict and resolution knows that the answer is the latter. The real heart of the story is in the connection you make when you tell a story. You are taking your audience on an emotional journey and guiding them along the way.

If you take the time to truly understand the emotional journey that your audience needs to be taken on, you will tell the right story. And if you adopt a storyteller's mindset of genuinely caring about your audience's agenda more than yours, you will tell it powerfully.

You can always learn more about storytelling

There is homework that you can do. Fortunately, it's the most enjoyable homework you've ever had. Your homework assignment is to watch stories, read stories and listen to stories. I'm sure you already do that. But now you will watch read and listen to them with a slightly different attitude and a little bit more knowledge. You will notice how they work and when they work well.

Learn from the best stories and bring the ideas and techniques you see in them back into your own presentations and documents.

Because the best story wins.

Notes

Introduction

1. K. A. Quesenberry and M. K. Coolsen, "What makes a Super Bowl ad super? Five-act dramatic form affects consumer Super Bowl advertising ratings", *Journal of Marketing Theory and Practice* 22(4) (2014), pp. 437–54.
2. K. A. Quesenberry and M. K. Coolsen, "Drama goes viral: effects of story development on shares and views of online advertising videos", *Journal of Interactive Marketing* 48(C) (2019), pp. 1–16.

Chapter 1: Why storytelling works

1. D. McCloskey and A. Klamer, "One quarter of GDP is persuasion", *American Economic Review* 85(2) (1995), pp. 191–5.
2. J. W. Brehm, *A Theory of Psychological Reactance* (Academic Press, 1966). Also, J. W. Brehm et al., "The attractiveness of an eliminated choice alternative", *Journal of Experimental Social Psychology* 2(3) (1966), pp. 301–13.
3. A. Damásio, *Descartes' Error: Emotion, Reason, and the Human Brain* (Putnam, 1994).
4. A. Bechara et al., "Deciding advantageously before knowing the advantageous strategy", *Science* 275(5304) (1997), pp. 1293–5.
5. M. S. Gazzaniga, *Tales from Both Sides of the Brain: A Life in Neuroscience* (Ecco Press, 2015).
6. J. S. Bruner, *The Process of Education* (Harvard University Press, 1960).
7. C. Heath and D. Heath, *Made to Stick: Why Some Ideas Survive and Others Die* (Random House, 2007).

Chapter 2: What is a story?

1. D. Mamet, *Three Uses of the Knife* (Columbia University Press, 1998).

2. B. Grebanier, *Playwriting: How to Write for the Theater* (Barnes & Noble, 1961).
3. J. Campbell, *The Hero with a Thousand Faces* (Pantheon, 1949).
4. C. Vogler, *The Writer's Journey: Mythic Structure for Writers* (Michael Wiese, 2007).
5. B. Snyder, *Save The Cat! The Last Book on Screenwriting That You'll Ever Need* (Michael Wiese, 2005).

Chapter 3: Storytelling at work
1. J. D. Leavitt and N. J. S. Christenfeld, "Story spoilers don't spoil stories", *Psychological Science* 22(9) (2011), pp. 1152–4.
2. A. Durayappah-Harrison, "The spoiler paradox: knowing a spoiler makes a story better, not worse", *Psychology Today* (August 22nd 2011).
3. P. Bailey, "Searching for storiness: story-generation from a reader's perspective", In: *Symposium on Narrative Intelligence* (AAAI Press, 1999).
4. D. Cooper, *Writing Great Screenplays for Film and TV* (Macmillan, 1994).
5. L. J. Silbert et al., "Coupled neural systems underlie the production and comprehension of naturalistic narrative speech," *Proceedings of the National Academy of Sciences* 111(43) (2014), pp. e4687–96.

Chapter 5: How to create great stories at work
1. "Sneezing baby panda": knowyourmeme.com/memes/sneezing-baby-panda
2. For more on "towards" and "away from", see S. R. Charvet, *Words That Change Minds: The 14 Patterns for Mastering the Language of Influence* (Kendall Hunt, 1997).

Chapter 6: Storytelling with data
1. H. Song and N. Schwarz, "If it's hard to read, it's hard to do: processing fluency affects effort prediction and motivation", *Psychological Science* 19(10) (2008), pp. 986–8.
2. E. R. Tufte, *The Visual Display of Quantitative Information* (Graphics Press, 1983).

3. N. Duarte, *Data Story: Explain Data and Inspire Action Through Story* (Ideapress, 2019).
4. W. S. Cleveland and R. McGill, "Graphical perception: theory, experimentation, and the application to the development of graphical methods", *Journal of the American Statistical Association* 79(387) (1984), pp. 531–54. Also, W. S. Cleveland, *Visualizing Data* (Hobart Press, 1993).
5. J. Gardner, *The Art of Fiction: Notes on Craft for Young Writers* (Alfred Knopf, 1984).

Chapter 8: The emotional journey
1. K. D. Elsbach and R. M. Kramer, "Assessing creativity in Hollywood pitch meetings: evidence for a dual-process model of creativity judgments", *Academy of Management Journal* 46(3) (2003). See also: R. Kramer, "What makes a successful pitch?", Stanford Business, Insights (April 15th 2003); and K. Elsbach,"How to pitch a brilliant idea", *Harvard Business Review* (September 2003).

Chapter 9: The writing process
1. K. Umejima et al., "Paper notebooks vs. mobile devices: brain activation differences during memory retrieval", *Frontiers in Behavioral Neuroscience* 15 (2021) 634158.
2. Virginia Berninger's findings are discussed in J. Schwarz, "The pen may be mightier than the keyboard", *University of Washington News* (September 16th 2009). This multi-pronged study involved senior author Kuniyoshi Sakai, a neuroscientist at the University of Tokyo, and his Sakai Lab members. For information on neuroscience, see "What is neuroscience?", *Psychology Today*.
3. "The reality is that the pulp, print and paper industry accounts for 1% of global greenhouse gas emissions, which makes the sector one of the lowest of all industrial emitters – half the emissions generated by those data centres." See "Is digital really greener than print?", pepper.co.uk
4. W. Strunk Jr and E. B. White, *The Elements of Style* (Harcourt, Brace & Howe, 1920).
5. G. Orwell, *Nineteen Eighty-four: The Facsimile of the Extant Manuscript* (Secker & Warburg, 1984).

Chapter 10: The stories you need to know

1. C. Booker, *The Seven Basic Plots: Why We Tell Stories* (Bloomsbury Continuum, 2004).
2. H. Schultz, *Onward: How Starbucks Fought for Its Life Without Losing Its Soul* (Harmony/Rodale, 2012).
3. "The man behind Starbucks reveals how he changed the world", *Bloomberg Originals* channel: www.youtube.com/watch?v=LnA7n9qSB7E
4. W. Isaacson, *Steve Jobs* (Simon & Schuster, 2011).
5. "Steve Jobs' 2005 Stanford Commencement Address" (with introduction by President John Hennessy), *Stanford* channel: www.youtube.com/watch?v=Hd_ptbiPoXM
6. "Spanx CEO Sara Blakely offers advice to redefine failure", *Insider Business* channel: www.youtube.com/watch?v=OZEPbyIA8XI
7. J. Bezos, "2017 Letter to shareholders", Amazon, April 19th 2018: www.aboutamazon.co.uk/news/company-news/2017-letter-to-shareholders
8. Indra Nooyi, PepsiCo Chairman and CEO, and Doug McMillon, Walmart President and CEO, on *Stanford Graduate School of Business* channel: www.youtube.com/watch?v=xl32J4TCSoE

Index

Index